CHESAPEAKE

NORFOLK

BEAUFORT

D0931761

PUBLISHED BY PEN & INK PRESS, P.O. BOX 235
WICOMICO CHURCH, VA 22579

PUBLISHER'S CATALOGING-IN-PUBLICATION
   (PROVIDED BY QUALITY BOOKS, INC.)

CARSTARPHEN, DEE
     NARROW WATERS : AN ARTIST'S MEMOIR OF SAILING THROUGH
SOUND, SWAMP, CITY, FOREST, MARSH, AND GLADE/ DEE
CARSTARPHEN. -- 1ST ED.
     P.   CM.
     INCLUDES BIBLIOGRAPHICAL REFERENCES.
     PREASSIGNED LCCN: 97-76110
     ISBN: 0-9607544-4-X

     1. SAILING -- ATLANTIC INTRACOASTAL WATERWAY. 2. ATLANTIC
INTRACOASTAL WATERWAY -- GUIDEBOOKS.   I. TITLE.

GV811.C37 1998   797.1'24'0975
                                  QBI97-41539

PRINTED IN THE UNITED STATES BY B&B PRINTING, RICHMOND, VA

NARROW
WATERS
by
Dee Carstarphen

Dedicated to
the Skipper

Introduction

This is the sketch log of a leisurely pleasure cruise, taken on a little sailboat. The boat is big enough for comfort, but small enough to handle easily. Her name is *Sea Wind*. She carries everything needed to be self-sufficient, allowing her crew to explore the narrow waters along the boundaries of land and sea, and live well as they do so.

Setting is the great, intricate waterway system of the eastern seaboard of the U.S., which brings together a myriad of natural water courses. Rivers and streams that drain into the Atlantic Ocean converge and cross. Canals shorten twisty rivers to link sounds, bays, tributaries, and creeks. Strong tides ebb and flood through the ocean inlets. These all join together to form the *Atlantic Intracoastal Waterway*. A boon to both commercial and pleasure craft alike, this watercourse runs behind the shore, or between the shore and islands, and is completely protected from the sea.

Technically, the waterway runs from Massachusetts Bay to Key West, Florida, with a connection via canals, rivers, and lakes to the west coast of Florida. However, north of Chesapeake Bay, the route inside the Jersey shore is too shallow for most boats, so the "waterway" is usually thought of as the section from Norfolk, Virginia, south — some 1,200 miles.

To cover this territory on the super-highway might take a couple of days. Brain-numb, perhaps,

FROM THE HOMOGENEOUS STRIP DEVELOPMENT; AN EXPERIENCE
YOU'RE GLAD TO FORGET. IT WILL TAKE *Sea Wind* A
COUPLE OF MONTHS, WHILE WE SAVOR THE RICH HARVEST OF
IMAGES AND ADVENTURES GLEANED FROM THE GRADUAL DESCENT
INTO THE DEEP SOUTH: CYPRESS, MAPLE, LIVE OAK, AND
SPANISH MOSS WILL GIVE WAY TO PALMETTO, PALM, SEA GRAPE,
AND MANGROVE; WILDLIFE WILL APPEAR IN THE STRETCHES
OF MARSH, SWAMP, FOREST, AND GLADE; WATERFRONT CITIES
LIKE NORFOLK, CHARLESTON, SAVANNAH, JACKSONVILLE,
AND MIAMI WILL OFFER A CHARMING AND COSMOPOLITAN
COUNTERPOINT.

THE SKETCH CHARTS IN THIS BOOK ARE FOR
INSPIRATION — NOT NAVIGATION.

FROST ON DECK. A NORTHER HAS PASSED THROUGH, AND THE FORECAST IS FOR NORTHWEST WINDS 15-20 KNOTS. A FIRE'S IN THE WOOD STOVE, AND HOT COFFEE'S WAITING. IT'S EXTRA SOCKS, WOOL HATS, AND WARM GLOVES TO GO ON DECK IN THE PRE-DAWN DARK, SET SAIL, RAISE THE ANCHOR, AND RUN OFF DOWN CHESAPEAKE BAY. TIME TO GO SOUTH. WE HAVE A BEAUTIFUL SAIL, PAST THE RAPPAHANNOCK AND THE YORK RIVERS, AROUND OLD PT. COMFORT — INTO THE BIG SHIPPING LANES AND ACROSS THE TRAFFIC COMING OUT OF THE JAMES RIVER.

A SUMMER ALONG THE MAINE COAST AND FALL SAILING ON THE CHESAPEAKE HAVE PRIMED US FOR THE INSIDE WATERS OF THE INTRACOASTAL

WATERWAY (I C W). HUNDREDS OF MILES OF PROTECTED
RIVERS, CANALS, BAYS, AND SOUNDS AWAIT. A GOOD
DEAL OF THE TIME THE SHORES WILL BE CLOSE ENOUGH
TO SUPPLY INTERESTING VIEWS – A LOT
OF UNDEVELOPED (AND SOME DEVELOPED)
COUNTRY. WHEN THE NORTHERS BLOW
THROUGH, *SEA WIND* CAN HOLE UP
IN THE PRE-FRONTAL BLASTS AND
SAIL SOUTH WHEN THE WIND SHIFT COMES.

WINTER SEAS MAY BE RAGING OUTSIDE OFF THE CAPES,
WE'LL BE SNUG AS A BUG IN THE I C W , SOMETIMES
MALIGNED AS THE "DITCH".

Hampton Roads
Hampton~Norfolk~Portsmouth~Newport News

SEA WIND SLIPS INTO THE ELIZABETH RIVER,
WITH A BACKWARDS GLANCE AT THE CHESAPEAKE AND
THE GOOD TIMES THERE – A
PENNY TOSSED INTO THE
WAKE FOR LUCK. A
ROLLY, BUT WELCOME
ANCHORAGE AWAITS US
BELOW HOSPITAL PT., UN-
EASY FROM WAKES, BUT
GOOD FOR A NIGHT'S REST.

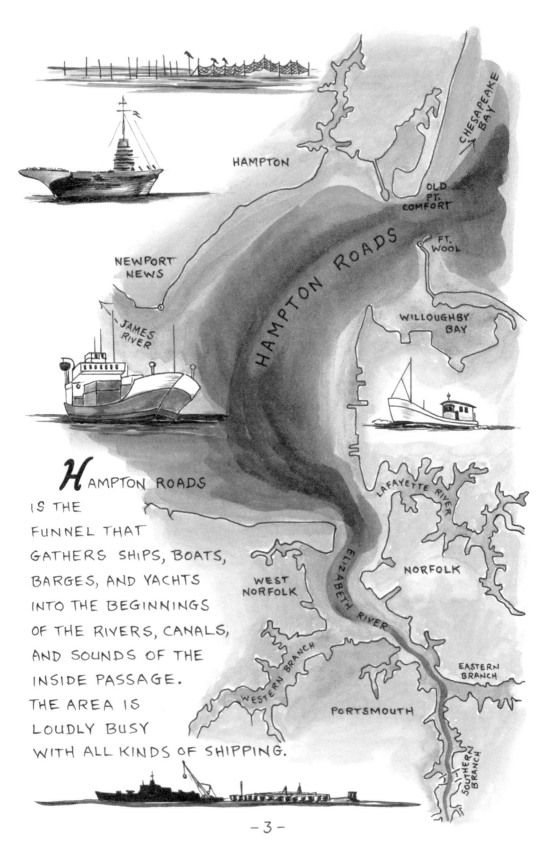

HAMPTON

CHESAPEAKE BAY

OLD PT. COMFORT

HAMPTON ROADS

FT. WOOL

NEWPORT NEWS

WILLOUGHBY BAY

JAMES RIVER

LAFAYETTE RIVER

NORFOLK

WEST NORFOLK

ELIZABETH RIVER

EASTERN BRANCH

WESTERN BRANCH

PORTSMOUTH

SOUTHERN BRANCH

*H*AMPTON ROADS IS THE FUNNEL THAT GATHERS SHIPS, BOATS, BARGES, AND YACHTS INTO THE BEGINNINGS OF THE RIVERS, CANALS, AND SOUNDS OF THE INSIDE PASSAGE. THE AREA IS LOUDLY BUSY WITH ALL KINDS OF SHIPPING.

THE NAVY IS EVERY-WHERE, WITH ANY STYLE OF HULL, BOW, OR STERN IMAGINABLE.

AT THE START, THIS WATERWAY BRINGS YOU IN TOUCH WITH THE THINGS A BIG CITY HAS TO OFFER, WHETHER YOU FANCY A CONCERT, OR JUST WANT TO

MANY CHURCH SPIRES — COPPER TOPS — ESPECIALLY ON THE PORTSMOUTH SIDE

SHOP. THE ELIZABETH RIVER IS FLANKED BY FIRST-CLASS WATERFRONT DEVELOPMENTS: "WATERSIDE" IN NORFOLK AND "PORTSIDE" IN PORTSMOUTH. THESE CITIES HAVE FOCUSED THEIR ATTENTION ON GIVING THE WATERBORNE TRAVELER EASY ACCESS. BOTH SHORES OFFER FREE TROLLEY TOURS AND TOURIST INFOR-MATION.

BILLY THE CAT SEES ALL

MILE 0 IS AT PORTSMOUTH.

(KEY WEST IS MILE 1240) * SOUTH OF THE CITY IS A KALEIDOSCOPE OF EXOTIC IN-DUSTRIAL SHAPES- DRY DOCKS, PIERS, PILES OF AGGRAGATE, CRANES, CONTAINER-SHIP TERMINALS, ALL LOOKING LIKE MONSTERS REARING ABOVE THE OCCASIONAL BRICK BUILDINGS OF YESTERYEAR, MONSTERS THEMSELVES IN THEIR TIME, NOW DWARFED, OUT OF PLACE.

THIS INDUSTRIAL COMPLEX SETS THE STAGE FOR ONE OF THE MOST DRAMATIC CHANGES ANY- WHERE ON THE WATERWAY, FOR ABRUPTLY, THE RIVER NARROWS AND YOU MOVE FROM HEAVY IN- DUSTRY WITH ALL ITS ACCOMPANYING SHRILL SOUNDS (AND SMELLS) TO ISOLATED STRETCHES AND WILD COUNTRY.

---

* THESE ARE STATUTE, OR LAND MILES, AS OPPOSED TO THE SAILOR'S CUSTOMARY NAUTICAL MILES. CURIOUSLY, FRESH AND INLAND WATERS ARE ALWAYS CHARTED IN STATUTE MILES. WHEN *SEA WIND'S* LOG READS 5 (N M) SHE WILL HAVE TRAVELED NEARLY 6 OF THESE LESSER MILES.

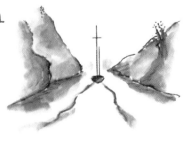

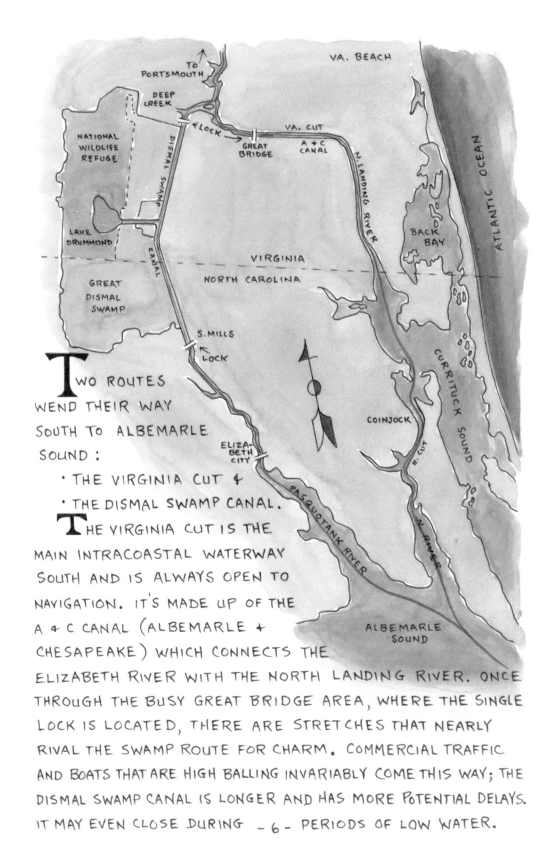

TWO ROUTES WEND THEIR WAY SOUTH TO ALBEMARLE SOUND :
· THE VIRGINIA CUT &
· THE DISMAL SWAMP CANAL.
THE VIRGINIA CUT IS THE MAIN INTRACOASTAL WATERWAY SOUTH AND IS ALWAYS OPEN TO NAVIGATION. IT'S MADE UP OF THE A & C CANAL (ALBEMARLE & CHESAPEAKE) WHICH CONNECTS THE ELIZABETH RIVER WITH THE NORTH LANDING RIVER. ONCE THROUGH THE BUSY GREAT BRIDGE AREA, WHERE THE SINGLE LOCK IS LOCATED, THERE ARE STRETCHES THAT NEARLY RIVAL THE SWAMP ROUTE FOR CHARM. COMMERCIAL TRAFFIC AND BOATS THAT ARE HIGH BALLING INVARIABLY COME THIS WAY; THE DISMAL SWAMP CANAL IS LONGER AND HAS MORE POTENTIAL DELAYS. IT MAY EVEN CLOSE DURING — 6 — PERIODS OF LOW WATER.

THE GREAT
DISMAL SWAMP

THE DISMAL SWAMP CANAL IS SOMETHING OF A RELIC. ITS WILD BEAUTY IS ENJOYED BY CRUISERS WHO AREN'T IN TOO MUCH OF A HURRY, AND WHOSE CRAFT DON'T DRAW TOO MUCH. THERE'S FASCINATING HISTORY HERE. THE GREAT DISMAL SWAMP — A WONDERFUL DARK NAME THAT BEFITS THE MANY TALES OF MYSTERY AND INTRIGUE ABOUT GHOSTS, FOXFIRE, SAVAGES, MOONSHINERS, AND DESPERATE FUGITIVES — QUICKSAND, POISONOUS PLANTS, SNAKES, AND WILD ANIMALS. THE SWAMP WAS A PLACE OF REFUGE FOR RUNAWAY SLAVES. TIMBER WAS THE REASON FOR CUTTING THE CANAL IN THE LATE 1700'S. GEORGE WASHINGTON SURVEYED THE SWAMP IN 1763. DUG BY SLAVES, IT TOOK TWELVE YEARS TO COMPLETE — TO A DEPTH OF ONLY TWO FEET. THROUGH THE YEARS IT WAS DEEPENED

AND ENJOYED PERIODS OF HARD USE, AND THEN NEGLECT
WHEN THE A AND C CANAL OPENED. THE U.S. GOVERN-
MENT PURCHASED THE DISMAL SWAMP CANAL FROM ITS
PRIVATE DEVELOPERS IN 1929 AND IN THE 70'S A LARGE
AREA OF THE SWAMP BECAME A FEDERAL WILDLIFE REFUGE.

TRANSITING THE CANAL ISN'T DISMAL AT ALL. IT'S A
LOVELY STRETCH — COLORFUL IN THE FALL, TREES FESTOONED
WITH MOSS AND MISTLETOE; FRESH AND GREEN WITH WILD
FLOWERS ALONG THE BANKS IN THE SPRING.

THE SWAMP'S A MASS OF ORGANIC MATERIAL WHICH HAS,
OVER THE CENTURIES, REACHED THE PEAT STAGE. THIS BUOYANT
MASS HAS RAISED THE SURFACE OF THE SWAMP IN THE MIDDLE,
NECESSITATING LOCKING VESSELS UP TO "SWAMP LEVEL"
AND THEN BACK DOWN TO SEA LEVEL AGAIN. THE PEAT
BEDS, IF THEY CATCH FIRE,
CAN BURN DOWN SEVERAL
FEET. IN 1923 A FIRE
DESTROYED 150 SQ. MILES
OF TIMBER IN THE SWAMP
AND THE PEAT LAND JUST
BURNED ON UNTIL 1926!
THE SWAMP'S
BEEN EXTENSIVELY
LUMBERED OVER.
FORTUNATELY,
THERE ARE STILL
AREAS HEAVILY
WOODED WITH
CYPRESS,
MAPLE,

OLD
CYPRESS
ROOT

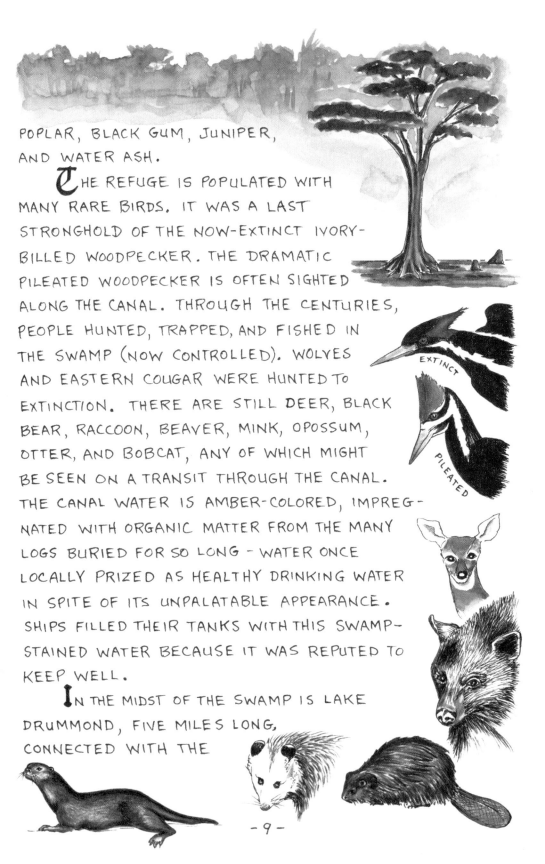

POPLAR, BLACK GUM, JUNIPER, AND WATER ASH.

THE REFUGE IS POPULATED WITH MANY RARE BIRDS. IT WAS A LAST STRONGHOLD OF THE NOW-EXTINCT IVORY-BILLED WOODPECKER. THE DRAMATIC PILEATED WOODPECKER IS OFTEN SIGHTED ALONG THE CANAL. THROUGH THE CENTURIES, PEOPLE HUNTED, TRAPPED, AND FISHED IN THE SWAMP (NOW CONTROLLED). WOLVES AND EASTERN COUGAR WERE HUNTED TO EXTINCTION. THERE ARE STILL DEER, BLACK BEAR, RACCOON, BEAVER, MINK, OPOSSUM, OTTER, AND BOBCAT, ANY OF WHICH MIGHT BE SEEN ON A TRANSIT THROUGH THE CANAL. THE CANAL WATER IS AMBER-COLORED, IMPREGNATED WITH ORGANIC MATTER FROM THE MANY LOGS BURIED FOR SO LONG – WATER ONCE LOCALLY PRIZED AS HEALTHY DRINKING WATER IN SPITE OF ITS UNPALATABLE APPEARANCE. SHIPS FILLED THEIR TANKS WITH THIS SWAMP-STAINED WATER BECAUSE IT WAS REPUTED TO KEEP WELL.

IN THE MIDST OF THE SWAMP IS LAKE DRUMMOND, FIVE MILES LONG, CONNECTED WITH THE

EXTINCT

PILEATED

CANAL BY A THREE-MILE FEEDER DITCH AT A PLACE TANTA-
LIZINGLY CALLED ARBUCKLE'S LANDING. THE LAKE WAS
NAMED FOR WILLIAM DRUMMOND, THE FIRST GOVERNOR OF
NORTH CAROLINA (WHO WAS LATER HANGED FOR HIS SHARE
IN BACON'S REBELLION). THERE ARE A MULTITUDE OF
CYPRESS STUMPS AND SNAGS UNDER THE SURFACE OF THE
LAKE – LEFT BY LUMBERING OPERATIONS LONG AGO – HARD
ON BOAT PROPS. A SMALL BOAT WITH LESS THAN THREE FT.
OF DRAFT CAN GO TO THE HEAD OF THE FEEDER DITCH AND A
FREE ELECTRIC RAILWAY WILL LIFT IT OVER A SMALL LAND
BRIDGE AND INTO LAKE DRUMMOND.

AN INN NAMED "HALFWAY HOUSE" EXISTED IN THE EARLY 1800'S ON THE ROAD THAT PARAL- LELS THE CANAL, HALF IN NORTH CAROLINA AND HALF IN VIRGINIA. A STAGECOACH STOP BETWEEN EDENTON, N. CAROLINA AND WASHINGTON, D.C., IT WAS NOTORIOUS AS A GAMBLING HOUSE AND PLACE OF REFUGE WHERE FUGITIVES FROM VIRGINIA COULD REST ON THE N. CAROLINA SIDE AND VICE VERSA. LITERARY LEGEND (UNSUPPORTED) HAS IT THAT EDGAR ALLEN POE WROTE "THE RAVEN" WHILE STOPPING HERE.

South Mills

WAS ONCE KNOWN
AS "OLD LEBANON",
BUT RE-NAMED FOR
AN ANCIENT MILL AT
THE SOUTHERN END OF THE
DISMAL SWAMP CANAL. IT'S POSSIBLE
TO TIE UP TO THE BULKHEAD BETWEEN THE BASCULE BRIDGE AND
THE LOCK, HAVE A WALK IN THE LITTLE TOWN, AND PERHAPS PICK UP
A JAR OF LOCAL SWAMP HONEY. NOTHING IS CERTAIN WHEN MESSING
ABOUT IN SMALL BOATS, HOWEVER. NO AMOUNT OF HORN BLOWING
RAISES THE BRIDGE ATTENDANT, SO *SEA WIND* RETREATS AND
ANCHORS IN THE CANAL. IT'S NOT NORMAL PROCEDURE TO LIE
OVERNIGHT IN THE NAVIGABLE CHANNEL. ANYWHERE ELSE YOU'D
HAVE THE RISK OF BEING RUN DOWN. BUT THE LOCKS AT DEEP
CREEK AND SOUTH MILLS ARE CLOSED FROM DUSK UNTIL DAWN,
WHICH ISOLATES OUR ANCHORAGE FROM THROUGH TRAFFIC.

HERE WE'RE JOINED BY THE CUTTER *ONDINE* - A BELGIAN
FLAG AT HER STERN. WE HAD SEEN HER AT ANCHOR IN
PORTSMOUTH, THE MATE DOING ENERGETIC
CALISTHENICS IN THE COCKPIT. WE
SPEND THE EVENING
TALKING WITH PAUL
AND PIERRETTE
ABOUT BOATS AND
FARAWAY PLACES.
THE NEXT FEW DAYS
SEA WIND AND
ONDINE WILL TRAVEL
IN COMPANY, EXTENDING A CHANCE ENCOUNTER.

WE'RE READY AT THE BRIDGE BY 8 A.M., FORTIFIED WITH OATMEAL PANCAKES, SYRUP, BACON, AND LASHINGS OF COFFEE. A HEFTY BRIDGE KEEPER APPEARS ON TIME TO OPEN THE DRAW, THEN LUMBERS OFF TO CLIMB IN HIS TRUCK AND DRIVE DOWN TO BECOME THE LOCK KEEPER. HE LOWERS *SEA WIND* AND *ONDINE* INTO TURNER CUT AND SO WE PASS OUT OF THE DISMAL SWAMP. IT'S A BRIGHT MID-NOVEMBER MORNING, BUT DEAD CALM. THE OLD GRAY 4-91 PUSHES US ALONG, THROUGH THE PERFECT REFLECTIONS OF SOFT FALL COLORS — INTO THE PASQUOTANK RIVER. IMAGES — CYPRESS AND GUM TREES FESTOONED WITH MISTLETOE; KINGFISHERS FLASHING IN THE SUNLIGHT. WE PASS POSSUM QUARTER LANDING, LAMBS CORNER AND SHIPYARD LANDING, NAMES ON THE CHART THAT SPEAK OF FORMER COMMERCE. BEHIND GOAT ISLAND WE ANCHOR UP FOR LUNCH AND LOOK OVER CHARTS FOR CRUISING THE NEXT FEW DAYS. THE RIVER NOW TURNS AND WINDS ABOUT, PRESENTING ONE PRETTY SCENE AFTER ANOTHER. SUDDENLY, TWIN BASCULE BRIDGES HERALD THE

TOWN OF **Elizabeth City.**

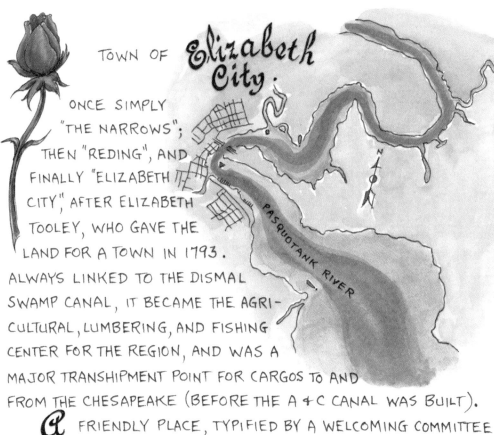

ONCE SIMPLY "THE NARROWS"; THEN "REDING", AND FINALLY "ELIZABETH CITY" AFTER ELIZABETH TOOLEY, WHO GAVE THE LAND FOR A TOWN IN 1793. ALWAYS LINKED TO THE DISMAL SWAMP CANAL, IT BECAME THE AGRICULTURAL, LUMBERING, AND FISHING CENTER FOR THE REGION, AND WAS A MAJOR TRANSHIPMENT POINT FOR CARGOS TO AND FROM THE CHESAPEAKE (BEFORE THE A & C CANAL WAS BUILT).

A FRIENDLY PLACE, TYPIFIED BY A WELCOMING COMMITTEE (APPROPRIATELY NAMED THE "ROSE BUDDIES"), WHO MEET VISITING YACHTS WITH A LONG-STEMMED ROSE, A PACKET OF LOCAL INFO, A LOG BOOK TO SIGN, AND A SMILE.

D OWN RIVER ON THE WEST SHORE ARE GIANT WORLD WAR II BLIMP HANGERS. ONE IS USED TO BUILD FURNITURE; THE OTHER IS OWNED BY A BLIMP COMPANY. THEY'RE VISIBLE FOR MILES.

G REY COMES THE MORNING, WITH TREES ALONG THE BANKS LIKE DARK SMOKE AGAINST THE SKY. RUST OF CYPRESS LEAVES, WITH A BIT OF YELLOW, ORANGE, AND RED FOR CONTRAST. WE SAIL AWAY EARLY, DOWN THE RIVER, BRUISING

WATER – 6 AND 7 KNOTS. A GOOD CHANCE TO CROSS ALBEMARLE SOUND, WITH THE POLE OUT– WING AND WING, *ONDINE* HARD ON OUR HEELS WITH HER SPINNAKER SET. THE VIRGINIA CUT AND DISMAL SWAMP ROUTES JOIN UP AT THE MOUTH OF THE **_Alligator River._**

THE BLOBS OF WHITE ON THE WATER AREN'T WHITECAPS, BUT A <u>LOT</u> OF SWANS. WHISTLING SWANS. THEY MIGRATE FROM THE ARCTIC IN THE FALL, FLYING AT GREAT HEIGHTS. SOME FOLLOW THE ATLANTIC COAST AND FIND RE-

FUGE ON THESE BROAD WATERS OF THE CAROLINAS. HERE, IN 1912, HENRY PLUMMER SAW A FLOCK OF MORE THAN A HUNDRED. (EVERY STAGE OF OUR WATERWAY CRUISE IS ACCOMPANIED BY READINGS FROM PLUMMER'S "THE BOY, ME AND THE CAT", ADVENTURES OF THE 24' CATBOAT *MASCOT* ON A VOYAGE FROM NEW BEDFORD, MASS. TO MIAMI AND BACK.)

THE BREEZE IS DYING. THE LITTLE ALLIGATOR RIVER IS CLOSE AT HAND AND THE CHART SHOWS WATER ENOUGH FOR OUR DRAFT. GIVING LONG SHOAL PT. PLENTY OF BERTH, *SEA WIND* WORKS IN BEHIND SANDY PT. TO FIND GOOD HOLDING IN 7 FT.

THERE'S JUST ENOUGH DAYLIGHT LEFT TO ROW ASHORE,

EXAMINE AN ABANDONED SHRIMPER IN THE WEEDS, STRETCH
THE LEGS, AND PICK UP SOME DRIFTWOOD FOR THE STOVE. ALL
UP AND DOWN THE COAST FROM MAINE TO
FLORIDA, ONE SEES THE HALF-SUNKEN
REMAINS OF OLD BOATS LEFT TO ROT OUT
IN THE SHALLOW BACKWATERS. AS WE
ROW BACK,
WE'RE

TREATED TO A
SURREALISTIC
SUNSET - THE RED SUN GOING DOWN
BEYOND DEAD CYPRESS TREES - MANY
STUMPS STICKING UP OUT OF THE WATER, THE WHOLE WITH *SEA
WIND* SILHOUETTED IN THE MIDDLE GROUND.

We'VE WORKED UP A FIERCE
APPETITE. SUPPER IS SOY BEANS
(DONATED LAST SUMMER BY A CHESA-
PEAKE FARMER HARVESTING HIS CROP),
LACED WITH SLIVERS FROM A VIRGINIA
HAM. ONE OF THE PLEASURES OF WATERWAY
CRUISING IS BEING ABLE TO CAPITALIZE ON LOCAL
FARE. IT'S NICE TO LEAVE THE CHESAPEAKE WITH AN
OLD-TIME VIRGINIA HAM HUNG BEHIND THE COMPANIONWAY
LADDER. LIKEWISE A CANVAS BAG OF SOY BEANS. A SMOKE
CURED COUNTRY HAM WILL LAST A GOOD WHILE, TO BE USED
AS FLAVORING FOR BEAN, POTATO, CLAM, AND OYSTER DISHES;
OR CHOPPED IN THE MORNING SCRAMBLE. A VINEGAR-SOAKED
CLOTH OVER THE CUT SURFACE WILL KEEP DOWN THE MOLD.

the ALLIGATOR RIVER

RUNS 20 MILES TO THE SOUTH BEFORE BENDING WEST AND NARROWING. IT'S WIDE (3 MILES IN SOME PLACES). IT NO LONGER HARBORS ALLIGATORS (WE'LL MEET THE FIRST OF THOSE A FEW MILES FURTHER DOWN), BUT IT'S GOT A HIDDEN CREEK WE ANTICIPATE EXPLORING. AT DAWN A

SLIGHT MIST ON THE WATER, SWIRLING ABOUT THE STUMPS AND TWIGS, GIVES AN IMPRESSION OF SWAMP CREATURES OOZING BACK INTO THE BOG. WATER THE COLOR OF COFFEE AND YOU CAN'T SEE VERY FAR INTO IT. WE'RE HEADING FOR *Milltail Creek* ! LOCATED ON THE EAST SIDE OF THE ALLIGATOR RIVER, BELOW THE SWING BRIDGE, THE CREEK'S ENTRANCE IS UNMARKED AND DIFFICULT TO FIND, JUST A SLOT A FEW YARDS WIDE ON A FEATURELESS SHORE. IT'S A QUIET DAY — PERFECT FOR THIS ENTERPRISE, UNDER POWER. WOULDN'T WANT

THE ENTRANCE TO MILLTAIL CREEK (FROM INSIDE)

TO BE FOOLING AROUND THAT SHORE IF A GOOD
WIND AND CHOP WERE
PUSHING YOU.

OUTSIDE THE INTRACOASTAL
CHANNEL ARE LOTS OF SNAGS AND
PARTLY SUBMERGED LOGS TO WATCH
FOR. A NICK IN THE PROP COULD SPOIL
THE DAY. THERE ARE A NUMBER OF
STUMPS ACROSS THE ENTRANCE THAT WE
MUST EASE PAST. THE FIRST TIME *SEA WIND*
APPROACHED **Milltail Creek**, THE SKIPPER
ANCHORED OUTSIDE AND SOUNDED BEFORE PRO-
CEEDING. ONCE IN, THE CREEK ITSELF HAS
GOOD DEPTHS OF WATER. IT'S NARROW,
AND TREES OCCASIONALLY OVERHANG THE
WAY. PART WAY UP WE SEE A HUNTING
CAMP, WITH A TOOTHLESS CARETAKER AND
A BUNCH OF HOUND DOGS THAT STARE AS YOU
PASS. WE MEET A FISHERMAN IN A JOHN BOAT.
IN THE 1950'S AN EX-CHESAPEAKE BUY BOAT,
THE *COASTAL QUEEN*, RUN BY SLADE DALE, TOOK
PAYING GUESTS UP AND DOWN THE WATERWAY. ONE
OF HIS FASCINATING INCIDENTS OF TRAVEL (RELATED
IN "THE INSIDE PASSAGE" BY ANTHONY BAILEY) WAS A
SIDE TRIP UP MILLTAIL CREEK, CARRYING THE COOK
ON TOP OF THE WHEEL HOUSE WITH A SAW TO LOP
OFF BRANCHES SO THEY COULD PROCEED. MORE
THAN ONE SAILBOAT'S RIGGING HAS ENTANGLED
A BRANCH OR TWO.

EAST
LAKE

LAUREL
PT.

RED
WOLF

BAY PT.

SAWYER LAKE

MILLTAIL
CREEK

FOUR MILES UP, THE CREEK OPENS INTO

COASTAL
QUEEN

SAWYER LAKE, WHERE BUFFALO CITY WAS ONCE LOCATED. IT WAS THE HEADQUARTERS FOR TIMBERING OPERATIONS, BUT WAS WIPED OUT BY A CHOLERA EPIDEMIC. THE CREEK WAS USED TO RUN LUMBER OUT BY BARGE. ALL THAT'S LEFT IS A BIT OF RUN-DOWN WHARFAGE AND SOME ROTTEN PILINGS. THE PROPERTY AROUND THE LAKE IS POSTED BY A LUMBER COMPANY. WE'RE GRATIFIED TO FIND IT

HASN'T BEEN NEWLY CUT OVER.* *SEA WIND* AND *ONDINE* ANCHOR OFF THE PILINGS. AN HOUR'S RUNNING DOWN THE LAKE IN THE DINK WITH THE OUTBOARD DOESN'T SHOW ITS EX-TENT. WE PLUCK A BIT OF MISTLETOE AND SPANISH MOSS TO HANG IN THE RIGGING. TOPSIDES IN THE EVENING, A BARRED OWL'S CALL REVERBERATES AROUND THE ANCHORAGE. NONE OF CIVILIZATION'S DISTRACTIONS HERE!

SEA WIND LAYS OVER, ENJOYING THE WILD ISOLATION AND CATCHING UP ON THE VARNISH, WHILE *ONDINE* MOVES ON.

*
THIS WHOLE AREA IS NOW PART OF THE "ALLIGATOR RIVER NATIONAL WILDLIFE REFUGE". THE HUNTING CAMP HAS BEEN RELOCATED. THE REFUGE IS SO LARGE AND WILD IT IS REPUTEDLY ONE OF THE LAST STRONGHOLDS OF THE CAROLINA COUGAR. RED WOLVES HAVE BEEN INTRODUCED BY MANAGEMENT BIOLOGISTS. FUTURE LOGGING WILL BE CONTROLLED. AN EXCURSION UP MILLTAIL CREEK IS NOW MORE APPEALING THAN EVER FOR A BOAT INTERESTED IN A WILD AND UN-SPOILED HABITAT.

Alligator River to Beaufort

THE SMALL-SCALE CHART SHOWS THE EXTENT OF SHALLOW ALBEMARLE AND PAMLICO SOUNDS, BOUND BY THE CHAIN OF ISLANDS KNOWN AS THE OUTER BANKS. NOTORIOUS CAPE HATTERAS JUTS OUT INTO THE ATLANTIC WITH TREACHEROUS DIAMOND SHOALS' SHIFTING SANDS LYING OFFSHORE. ALTHOUGH RESPECTED BY SEAMEN FOR ITS BRUTAL WEATHER, IT HAS NEVERTHELESS EARNED THE NICKNAME "GRAVEYARD OF THE ATLANTIC".

SIX DROWNED CYPRESS TRAILING OFF TUCKAHOE PT. FRAME AN EVENING'S ANCHORAGE. A LARGE OSPREY NEST DECORATES THE OUTERMOST. A GAUDY SUNSET LIGHTS THE ENTRANCE TO THE ALLIGATOR-PUNGO CANAL ON THE OPPOSITE SHORE.

THE CANAL JOINING THE *Alligator* AND *Pungo* RIVERS IS ARROW-STRAIGHT. NOTES ON THE SIDE OF THE CHART SUGGEST YOU STAY IN THE MIDDLE, A DIFFICULT THING TO DO WHEN A TUG WITH BARGE COMES ALONG. THE BANKS ARE ERODED DUE TO CONSTANT WAKES AND ARE LINED WITH A LOT OF SNAGS. THE SKIPPER, PERHAPS WITH A STREAK OF TOM SAWYER IN HIM, ELECTS A MORE CHALLENGING ALTERNATE ROUTE, THE WILD WINDING ALLIGATOR RIVER. THE OLD, NATURAL WATERWAY HAS BEEN LEFT TO ITSELF. SOME SECTIONS ARE DESOLATE AND PARTS ARE BURNED OVER. THE POINTS ARE BESET WITH STUMPS. IT'S TORTUOUS WITH PLENTY OF TWISTS AND TURNS. HUNTING HAWKS RANGE ABOVE THE TREES. WHEN WE FINALLY NEAR THE ICW ONCE MORE, WE TUCK IN BEHIND A SMALL GRASSY ISLET IN A LITTLE LOOP OF THE RIVER AND DROP THE HOOK. WE'RE CLOSE ENOUGH TO SEE THE UPPER WORKS OF BOATS PASSING IN THE CANAL, BUT SNUG IN OUR MINI-SPOT OF SOLITUDE.

RED-SHOULDERED HAWK

ALLIGATOR RIVER

ALLIGATOR-PUNGO CANAL

THE SKIPPER

-20-

Thanksgiving—

FOGGY EDGES OF OUR MARSHY WORLD ARE JUST VISIBLE. BY THE SECOND CUP OF COFFEE IT'S CLEARED AND WE'VE WORKED OUR WAY BACK INTO THE INTRACOASTAL. SOON LAYERS OF COATS AND SWEATERS COME OFF. A MINCE PIE BAKES AS WE GO. YEAST ROLLS ARE RISING. *SEA WIND* SLIDES ALONG, COURTESY OF ENGINE, MAIN, AND MULE. IN THE PUNGO RIVER, SUDDENLY THE MARKERS REVERSE. STRANGE TO LEAVE THE GREEN TO STARBOARD. STUDYING THE CHART, WE CONCLUDE ITS BECAUSE WE'RE SHARING A CHANNEL CARRYING TRAFFIC FROM SEAWARD AND SUCH CHANNELS ARE ALWAYS BUOYED "RED RIGHT RETURNING". THEY'LL STAY THIS WAY UNTIL SOUTH OF THE PAMLICO RIVER.

*B*UT FOR OURS TODAY IS TO ANCHOR EARLY, EXPLORE, AND MAKE A FEAST. *SEA WIND* TURNS TO STARBOARD AND SNEAKS INTO AN UNNAMED CREEK.

MARKERS REVERSE HERE GOING DOWN THE PUNGO

PUNGO RIVER

𝕴N THE SHALLOWS LIE THE BONES OF AN OLD SAILING VESSEL. CLAMS ARE BURIED IN THE MUD. WE SCULL ABOUT THE MARSHES, THE WRECK, AND TAKE A WALK IN THE WOODS. A GNARLY LITTLE TREE SURRENDERS A COUPLE OF WALKING STICKS. THE MARSHES GIVE UP EIGHT CLAMS (SIX FOR US AND TWO FOR THE CAT). THEN TO THE REAL BUSINESS OF THE DAY. WE MUZZLE INTO BAKED HAM, STUFFING WITH HOMINY AND CLAMS, ASPARAGUS TIPS, FRESH BAKED ROLLS, AND OUR MINCE PIE, TOPPED OFF WITH A SPECIAL BOTTLE OF ROSÉ.

𝕬 LIGHT SOUTHEASTERLY GIVES US A SAIL TO BELHAVEN. ALONG THE WAY: ONE TRAWLER YACHT CAUTIOUSLY SLOWS FOR EVERY WAKE, TURNING TO CROSS AT RIGHT ANGLES, SOMETIMES COMPLETING A FULL CIRCLE TO DO SO. ON THE VHF EVERY FEW MINUTES HE EXHORTS BOATS TO PLEASE PASS THEM SLOWLY. EITHER THE CROCKERY IS LOOSE, OR AN ANGEL FOOD CAKE IS BAKING.

HOOOOO—
CALL OF THE
LONG-EARED OWL
IN THE NIGHT.

A SMALL SAILBOAT POWERS BY, THE COUPLE IN THE COCKPIT SWATHED IN BLUE VEILS. ARE THEY READING THE ARABIAN NIGHTS? ON THE LAM? OR JUST HIDING FROM THE SUN?

BLUE HEAVEN

GARDEN SCRATCHER, WITH HOME-MADE HANDLE, FOR CLAMMING.

BELHAVEN

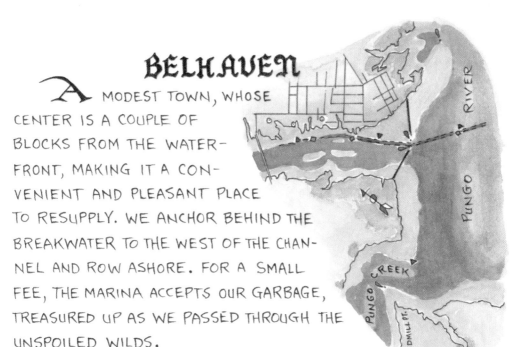

A MODEST TOWN, WHOSE CENTER IS A COUPLE OF BLOCKS FROM THE WATER- FRONT, MAKING IT A CON- VENIENT AND PLEASANT PLACE TO RESUPPLY. WE ANCHOR BEHIND THE BREAKWATER TO THE WEST OF THE CHAN- NEL AND ROW ASHORE. FOR A SMALL FEE, THE MARINA ACCEPTS OUR GARBAGE, TREASURED UP AS WE PASSED THROUGH THE UNSPOILED WILDS.

THIS HARBOR CAN BE CHOPPY IN THE PRE- DICTED SOUTHERLY (DESPITE THE BREAKWATERS). ALTHOUGH NEARBY PUNGO CREEK WOULD OFFER BETTER PROTECTION BEHIND WINDMILL PT., *SEA WIND* OPTS TO SLIP FURTHER DOWN THE RIVER TO SLADE CREEK. THE ENTRANCE IS WIDE BUT WITH UNMARKED SHOALS ON EACH SIDE, SO IT'S PRUDENT TO TAKE A COMPASS COURSE GOING IN. AROUND THE FIRST BEND IS A LOVELY ANCHORAGE IN THE MOUTH OF NEAL CREEK. NO HOUSES. IT FEELS REMOTE. WE'RE VISITED BY A MAN FROM THE NORTH CAROLINA WILDLIFE MANAGEMENT. HE'S BASED IN SWAN QUARTER AND CHECKS THINGS OUT BY OUTBOARD. A LOT OF THE SURROUNDING PROPERTY BELONGS TO A TIMBER CO.

THE BAROMETER FORETELLS A COLD FRONT. *SEA WIND* PROFITS FROM THE PRE-FRONTAL SOU'WESTERLY BY SAILING ON A CLOSE REACH DOWN THE PUNGO. WHERE IT EMPTIES INTO THE **PAMLICO RIVER**, WE HEAD NORTHWEST, HOPING TO REACH THE PROTECTION OF BATH CREEK BEFORE THE FRONT AND ITS COLDER WEATHER. IT'S A GRAND SAIL TO START, BUT PART WAY UP THE PAMLICO, THE SKY TURNS DARK, THE WIND YEERS, COMES GUSTY, AND RAISES SHORT, STEEP WHITE-CAPS. THE NORTHWEST WIND AND AN ADVERSE CURRENT FORCE A WET, COLD THRASH TO A WELCOME ANCHOR-AGE ACROSS FROM THE TOWN DOCK. CANADA GEESE IN THE SHALLOWS — SOME HONKING. WE THROW STALE BREAD ON THE WATER, BUT THEY ARE NOT IN-TERESTED. THE SEA GULLS ARE.

BATH

BATH CREEK

PAMLICO RIVER

Bath IS THE OLDEST TOWN IN NORTH CAROLINA; SETTLED BY FRENCH HUGUENOTS IN THE LATE 1600'S. VERY QUIET AND VERY SMALL, IT BOASTS A FEW HISTORIC BUILDINGS AS WELL AS AN ASSOCIATION WITH BLACK-BEARD THE PIRATE.

*T*HE PAMLICO RIVER IS WIDE AND
DEEP WITH WOODED SHORES. LOTS OF
DUCK BLINDS (COMPLETE WITH HUNTERS
AT THIS TIME OF YEAR,
THEIR DECOYS SCATTERED AROUND). THE
WEATHER COMES
CLEAR AND COLD
AND THE WIND DROPS. THE CABIN IS COZY, WARM FROM THE
WOOD STOVE. WE'VE EATEN OUR OATMEAL LACED WITH BROWN
SUGAR AND RAISINS, AND HAD OUR RATION OF COFFEE. IT'S TIME
TO GO SAILING! BUT NOT FOR
LONG, AND NOT FAR.

PAMLICO RIVER

COUSIN PT.

CHAMBERS PT.

ROSS CREEK

TEN MILES BELOW BATH,
SITUATED ON THE NORTH SIDE OF THE RIVER, IS THE EN-
TRANCE TO SOME ATTRACTIVE CREEK COUNTRY. WE ENTER
BETWEEN COUSIN PT. AND CHAMBERS PT. THROUGH A RATHER
NARROW CHANNEL, AND FIND A TIDY AND DELIGHTFUL SPOT TO
ANCHOR WEST OF THE ENTRANCE TO ROSS CREEK. IT'S MUF-
FLER AND MITTY WEATHER BUT THE SUN IS WARM IN THE
MARSHES. AN AFTERNOON FOR INTROSPECTION AND PICKING
UP FALLEN WOOD ALONG THE SHORE TO FEED THE TINY TOT.
*G*UNSHOTS ROUSE US OUT AT DAYBREAK: THE HUNTERS
ARE OUT. WE REVERSE YESTERDAY'S COMPASS COURSES AND

REJOIN THE WATERWAY ONCE MORE. GOOSE CREEK. MOST PLEASING AND INTERESTING COUNTRY. A LOOK AT THE CHART SHOWS MANY POSSIBLE ANCHORAGES.

SEA WIND CARRIES ON, HOWEVER, PAST THE HOBUCKEN SWING BRIDGE. HERE ARE DOCKS WHERE WORKING SHRIMPERS AND SMALL FREIGHTERS TIE UP. ONE OLD DEAR NAMED *GOD'S MERCY* CATCHES OUR EYE. WE COME TO REST FOR THE NIGHT IN GALE CREEK JUST OUTSIDE THE WATERWAY CHANNEL TO THE WEST OF MARKER #23. THIS IS A MARSHY CORNER; ONE HOUSE IN VIEW. SHELL-FISH POLLUTION SIGNS KEEP US FROM POKING AMONG THE GRASSES FOR OYSTERS. A SMALL CUTTER SETTLES NEARBY, NAME OF *SILVERHEELS*, OUT OF CHICAGO. OUT WITH THE RIDING LIGHT, TO MARK OUR PRESENCE FOR BOATS TRAVELING THE WATERWAY AT NIGHT. WHEN THE WIND IS UP, ESPECIALLY IF IT'S FROM THE EAST, IT CAN BE A ROUGH

GALE CREEK

'22

'23

'24' '25'

BAY RIVER

R.R. LANTERN ANCHOR LIGHT

GOD'S MERCY
LOWLAND
N.C.

GO HEADING INTO THE **Bay River** AND AROUND **Maw Pt.** FROM HERE THERE'S A THIRTY MILE FETCH TO THE OUTER BANKS. IT APPEALS TO US TO MAKE AN EXCURSION TO THOSE BARRIER ISLANDS AND VISIT OCRACOKE, BUT THE WEATHER IS TOO UNSETTLED. IT WILL KEEP FOR ANOTHER TIME. WE SAIL OFF THE ANCHOR WITH LIGHT ENOUGH AIRS FOR THE SKIPPER TO SET THE MULE TO HELP US ALONG. ONCE IN THE **Neuse River**, THINGS PICK UP, AND SOON *SEA WIND* IS SURFING ALONG WITH THE JIB OUT ON THE POLE. A ROARING RUN, DEAD DOWNWIND WITH THE DINGHY SLEWING WILDLY AROUND ON ITS PAINTER. IN RETROSPECT, WE WISH WE'D TAKEN THE LITTLE BOAT ABOARD BEFOREHAND. THE NEUSE KICKS UP A GOOD CHOP TOO AND IN THESE OPEN WATERS WE KEEP CHECKING MARKERS ASTERN AS WELL AS AHEAD. WIND AND TIDE SET YOU ONE WAY OR THE OTHER AND IN SOME PLACES THE SHOALS CREEP OUT VERY NEAR THE

ORIENTAL
TOWN DOCK

MARKERS. TIME TO STRIKE THE MULE WHEN WE HARDEN UP
TO ENTER THE CHANNEL AT ORIENTAL.

THIS NORTH CAROLINA TOWN LIES ON THE NORTH-
WEST SIDE OF THE
NEUSE RIVER AND
HAS A LITTLE HAR-
BOR SITUATED
BEHIND A ROCK
BREAKWATER.
THERE'S A
SMALL DOCK
WHERE YOU
CAN TIE UP,
COURTESY OF THE TOWN. WE TAKE ON FUEL AND WATER AT
THE MARINA, BUT CHOOSE TO GO 'ROUND TOWARDS THE BRIDGE
TO ANCHOR JUST OUTSIDE THE ENTRANCE CHANNEL. THERE'S NOT
TOO MUCH DEPTH, DUE TO A FEW DAYS OF WINDS FROM THE
NORTHEAST BLOWING DOWN THE NEUSE. LOWER LEVELS THAN
THE CHART INDICATES, BUT ENOUGH FOR OUR 4.5 FT. DRAFT. A
FEW SHRIMPERS MAKE ORIENTAL PICTURESQUE. THE OLD, WELL-
KEPT HOMES ASHORE ADD TO THE CHARM. POST OFFICE, GROCERY,
AND A RESTAURANT ARE AN EASY WALK. BACK ABOARD WE
DECIDE TO SAIL FURTHER.

WE CROSS THE NEUSE UNDER ALL PLAIN
SAIL TO ADAMS CREEK AND MAKE ALONG TO
THE JUNCTURE OF CEDAR AND JONAQUIN
CREEKS, FURLING SAIL AS WE GO, TO SET
THE HOOK IN 6 FT. EAST OF MARKER # "9". THE
LATE AFTERNOON HAS TURNED INTO A MOOD
PIECE, WITH THE SKY AND SEA SHADES OF

GUN METAL. THE WATER LOOKS LIKE THE WOOD STOVE AFTER
IT'S POLISHED. IT'S GOOD TO GO
BELOW AND BUILD THE
LITTLE FIRE, SUP OUR
CHICKEN SOUP, AND RE-
LAX, BUT NOT FOR LONG,
DUE TO THE VISIT OF A
COAST GUARD HELIOCOPTER,
DRIVING SPRAY ALL OVER
US, HOVERING CLOSE ABOVE,
APPARENTLY TRYING TO
COMMUNICATE. FINALLY
THE PILOT INFORMS US, VIA
V H F, THAT THEY'RE LOOKING FOR A BLACK SAILBOAT NAMED
PELICAN THAT'S GONE MISSING.

U P CEDAR CREEK IS A SEAFOOD PRO-
CESSING PLANT WHERE YOU CAN GET SHRIMP,
SCALLOPS, CRAB, OR FLOUNDER, DEPENDING ON WHAT'S BEEN BROUGHT
IN BY THE LOCAL FISHERMEN THAT MORNING. NOON IS A GOOD TIME
TO INQUIRE, BEFORE THE DAY'S CATCH HAS BEEN TRUCKED AWAY. IT'S
A CLEAN PLANT AND THE FOLKS ARE FRIENDLY TO A DINGHY COMING IN
TO THEIR DOCKS. TO THE NORTHEAST, UP JONAQUIN CREEK, IS A
FARM WHERE YOU CAN BUY PRODUCE IN
SEASON, AND
HELP PICK IT.
ONCE, IN
JUNE, WE CAME AWAY
WITH BROWN EGGS, NEW POTATOES, BEETS, GREEN BEANS,
SQUASH, LETTUCE, CUKES, ONIONS, APPLES, AND PEACHES,
ALL FRESH FROM THE CHICKEN, EARTH, OR TREE. PLUS A

BONUS BOUQUET OF COLORFUL CUT FLOWERS.
*A*N ABSOLUTELY PEARLY DAWN, WITH
PINK OVER-
TONES AND
RIBBONS OF MIST
LOW IN THE MARSHY PLACES. LET'S GO, LET'S GO! DESTINA-
TION BEAUFORT, ALL OF TWELVE MILES
AWAY. WE SIGHT MR. RACKETY COON
ON A LOG IN CORE CREEK CANAL.
HE TRIES TO SCRAMBLE UP THE
BANK, BUT IS SO FAT, HE FALLS BACK
AND JUST WATCHES US PASS. A LITTLE
FURTHER ON WE'RE TREATED TO A RIVER
OTTER SWIMMING ALONG
THE SHORE. WE
FIND CLAM
DREDGERS AT WORK
NEAR THE CORE CREEK BRIDGE. BARGE-LIKE BOATS THEY
ARE. ON THROUGH GALLANT CHANNEL AND
THE BASCULE BRIDGES
INTO TAYLOR CREEK
AND BEAUFORT'S WATER-
FRONT. THE ANCHORAGE
OPPOSITE THE TOWN

DOCKS IS FULL OF YACHTS AND WHEN WE FIND A CRANNY,
SEA WIND SETS TWO HOOKS, BECAUSE OF THE REVERSING
TIDAL CURRENTS.

BEAUFORT, N.C. (BOFORT)

When Henry Plummer's *Mascot* arrived in Beaufort in 1912, she found a bustling town. Smacks anchored off the wharves and fish houses; an oyster-opening plant employed men, women, and children to open

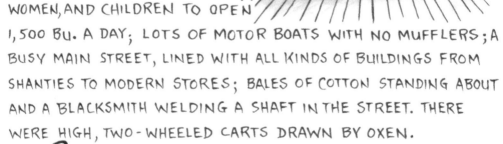

1,500 Bu. A day; lots of motor boats with no mufflers; a busy main street, lined with all kinds of buildings from shanties to modern stores; bales of cotton standing about and a blacksmith welding a shaft in the street. There were high, two-wheeled carts drawn by oxen.

At that time a boat proceeding south from Beaufort had to run out what Plummer described as a "twisting little gutter running between nasty shoals" to the ocean and sail along the beach to re-enter the inside route, such as it was, at Georgetown, South Carolina, with perhaps a stop at Southport, on the Cape Fear River.

Beaufort channel is today a deep inlet serving both Beaufort and nearby Moorehead City, seaports for foreign and coastal trade. Beaufort draws the yachts, while Moorehead City is more a commercial and sport-fishing center.

After Henry Plummer's era, Beaufort fell on hard times and as late as the 70's the waterfront was an unappealing stop for yachts. Then the city turned it's face to

IT'S HARBOR AND REBUILT THE MAIN STREET. SOME OF THE OLD
HOMES DATING FROM THE 17 AND 1800'S WERE RESTORED. THERE'S
LONGSIDE DOCKAGE AND A DINGHY FLOAT FOR THOSE ANCHORED OUT.
SHOPS, RESTAURANTS, MARINE STORES, AND SUPPLIES ARE AVAIL-
ABLE. BEST OF ALL, A MARINE MUSEUM HAS INTERESTING
EXHIBITS, A BOOK STORE SELLING MARINE BOOKS AND CHARTS,
AND A GOOD LIBRARY OF SEA AND NATURE-ORIENTED BOOKS.
IT EVEN OFFERS BOAT TRAVELLERS THE USE OF A CAR OR BICYCLE.

THE RED CUTTER *NORDLYS* IS HERE, PREPARING FOR AN
OFFSHORE VOYAGE. CANADIANS ED AND NANCY. ED SPENT YEARS
BUILDING HIS STRIP-PLANKED BOAT WITH A VIEW TO A WORLD
CRUISE. THE SKIPPER FIRST MET ED YEARS AGO IN THE
BAHAMAS, SO WE MUST GET TOGETHER TO CATCH UP AND EX-
CHANGE NEWS OF MUTUAL BOATING FRIENDS. THEY'RE HEADING
OFFSHORE FROM BEAUFORT TO THE CARIBBEAN.

WIERD AND WONDERFUL LOOKING YACHTS, ALONG WITH TRADI-
TIONAL ONES POPULATE THE ANCHORAGE. *SEA WIND* STAYS A FEW
DAYS, TAKING CARE OF BOAT CHORES, VISITING, AND WANDERING ASHORE.
THE BURYING GROUND CATCHES OUR FANCY. ONE QUAINT TALE TELLS
OF A GIRL WHO, RETURNING FROM A VISIT TO OLD ENGLAND, PERISHED
AT SEA. HER FATHER HAD PROMISED TO BRING HER HOME AND SO HE
DID, PRESERVED IN A CASK OF THE SHIP'S RUM.

WE TAKE A RAMBLE ON CARROT ISLAND, WHERE THERE'S
A SMALL BAND OF WILD HORSES, AND BREATHE
IN THE TANGY SEA SMELL—

MISSED DURING ALL
THE INLAND WATER-
WAY WORK.

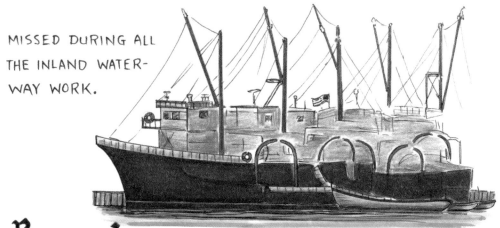

Beaufort Impressions:

- THE MENHADEN FLEET TIED UP AT THE NORTHWEST END OF TOWN.
- A GROUP OF (PROBABLY STONED) YOUTHS TEARING THROUGH THE ANCHORAGE IN A SPEED BOAT SCREAMING OBSCENITIES AS THEY GO.
- A COUPLE ROWING A TINY DINGHY ASHORE IN A GALE.
- CRUISE SHIP AT THE TOWN DOCK WITH HER GENERATOR RUNNING FAR INTO THE NIGHT.
- NEARBY POWER BOAT WITH EXOTIC COUPLE LIVING ABOARD. MAN SPORTS LAVENDER PANTS, YELLOW SHIRT, AND CAPTAIN'S HAT. HIS LADY WITH A LONG GOWN AND BRAID. BOAT'S NAME *BISMI ILAHI R-AHMANI R-AHIM*, PORT "PASHTUNISTON". A LARGE BLACK BUG INSIGNIA, A BLACK FLAG, AND BLACK DINGHY.
- BILLY THE CAT SITTING ON DECK IN THE FOG STARING AT SOME- THING WE CAN'T SEE, FUR BEADED WITH MOISTURE.

Beaufort to Charleston

The waterway now runs past inlets with strong cross-currents, through shallow sounds and salt marshes. Sand dunes show occasionally, built up by years of seas pounding in from the open Atlantic. A cut through higher land with wooded banks leads to the lovely Waccamaw River, past Georgetown into Winyah Bay. Then new swamp-lands, rivers, and inlets to traverse until our water way leads us into the heart of Charleston.

Leave Beaufort at dawn one morning; the sky blood red; soon turns pink and orange. Flights of cormorants and skimmers are wheeling above. We run out of Beaufort with the fishing boats, but turn west at the juncture of Moorehead City channel. It's good to be under way again.

$\mathcal{D}$OWN BETWEEN THE SPOIL ISLANDS AND THE MAINLAND —
Bogue Sound – TRAILING A FISHING LINE. WE CATCH A
SMALL BLUEFISH WHICH MR.
BILL SAYS SHOULD BE
<u>HIS</u>. IN SPITE OF
A FAVORABLE CUR-
RENT, THE FITFUL BREEZE IS

THE VORACIOUS BLUE

SO LIGHT WE DOUSE SAIL AND POWER TO **Swansboro**. WE
WALK THE QUIET OLD TOWN AND TAKE A DINGHY
EXPLORE AROUND NEARBY HUGGINS ISLAND.
VISIBLE ACROSS THE INLET ARE THE GRASS-
CAPPED SAND DUNES ON BOGUE
BANKS. BACK ABOARD TO FINISH
THE DAY WITH A SMALL BEEF ROAST.
(BILLY GETS THE FISH AFTER ALL.)

SWANSBORO HIGHWAY BRIDGE

$\mathcal{A}$ FOGGY, VERY EARLY START, TO MAKE IT SAFELY PAST
A STRETCH THAT CUTS
THROUGH THE MARINE
CORPS' CAMP LE JEUNE,
WHICH WE LEARNED IN
SWANSBORO WOULD BE CLOSED TO TRAFFIC BY 8 A.M. FOR

WARNING—
NEXT 4 MI.
DO NOT LAND
IMPACT AREA

FIRING EXERCISES. WE HAVE THE HIGH SPIRITS
(ONLY TEMPORARILY DAMPENED WHILE *SEA
WIND* TRAVELS BETWEEN THE HIDDEN GUNS)
OFTEN FELT WITH AN EARLY START. THE
MISTY MARSH SCENES
ARE GRAND. WE SIGHT PORPOISES NEAR
NEW RIVER INLET. THE FOG PERSISTS—

BECOMES THICK AS PEA SOUP. *SEA WIND* FEELS HER WAY
INTO MILE HAMMOCK BAY, A DREDGED BASIN (MARINE CORPS'
PROPERTY ASHORE). WHILE WE BRUNCH ON HAM, EGGS,
AND GRITS, THE FOG THINS, LETTING US SAIL SOME TWENTY
MILES THROUGH ALLIGATOR BAY AND
STUMP SOUND.

STREAMERS OF FOG ACCOMPANY US
AS WE FOLLOW A MARKED CHANNEL TO
PORT OUT ALONG **Topsail Beach**,
WHERE WE ANCHOR SNUGLY IN THE LEE OF
A SMALL ISLAND. THERE'S JUST TIME TO
PICK A BUCKETFUL OF
OYSTERS (PLUS THREE

LARGE QUAHOGS) IN
THE SHALLOWS BE-
FORE THE FOG SOCKS
IN SOLIDLY.

COME MORNING,
STILL FOG-BOUND. WE
SPEND THE DAY AT
ANCHOR, WRAPPED IN
COTTON WOOL.
Wrightsville Beach, TO
THE SOUTH, IS BRISTLING WITH CONSTRUCTION AND YACHT
FACILITIES. IN CONTRAST, **Myrtle Grove Sound** TREATS US TO
A GLUT OF BIRD SIGHTINGS: BLACK-NECKED STILT, LITTLE
BLUE HERON, GREAT BLUE HERON, GREAT EGRET, WHITE
IBIS, KINGFISHER, LOUISIANA HERON,

- 36 -

AND OYSTER CATCHER — WE
NOTE THEM ALL.

THE CURRENT IS FAVORABLE
THROUGH SNOWS CUT AND FOR RUNNING
DOWN THE **Cape Fear River**. A
CHANCE! IF THE TIDE IS WRONG
HERE, THIS PASSAGE WOULD BE
SLOW, WEARY WORK. WE MOVE
SMARTLY ALONG — DOWN, DOWN
IN THE SHIP CHANNEL WITH
WIDER VIEWS AND BROADER
HORIZONS. AFTER *SEA WIND*
SLIPS BACK INTO NARROWER
CONFINES AT SOUTHPORT, SHE
NOSES HER WAY INTO **Dutch-
man Creek** TO SPEND A
QUIET NIGHT. FORTY SEVEN
MILES ON THE LOG, A LONGISH
DAY'S RUN FOR US. IT'S
WARM ENOUGH FOR COCK-
PIT SHOWERS. A PLASTIC GARDEN
SPRAY WITH HOSE AND NOZZLE LIVES
IN A LOCKER NEXT TO THE ENGINE
EXHAUST. TODAY'S
LONG POWER
RUN HAS WARMED
THAT LOCKER CON-
SIDERABLY, RE-
SULTING IN HOT
SHOWERS.

THE WATERWAY NOW LEADS US ACROSS INLETS AND BE-
HIND DUNES AND COASTAL SWAMPS. THE OCEAN BEACHES ARE
VERY BUILT UP WITH STILT HOUSES; ALL KINDS OF SPINDLY ARCHI-
TECTURAL SHAPES STARK AGAINST THE SKY. BRAVE INDEED, FOR
THIS IS A HURRICANE COAST.

WE CROSS LOCKWOOD'S FOLLY INLET. THE NAME IS RECORDED
ON A 1671 CHART, AND REFERS TO LOCKWOOD'S FOOLHARDINESS
IN FOUNDING A SETTLEMENT SO EXPOSED TO BOTH SEA AND
INDIANS, BY WHOM IT WAS PROMPTLY DESTROYED. SHALLOTTE,
TUBBS AND MAD INLET PRESENT US WITH LOTS OF SHIFTY-LOOKING
BARS AND CHANNELS. IT'S STARTING TO RAIN AND **Calabash
Creek** OFFERS. WE'RE IN SOUTH CAROLINA NOW. *SEA WIND*
FINDS TEN FT. OF WATER ON THE MAINLAND SIDE BY A WOODED
SHORE. THE SALMON TRAWLER *CHINOOK* COMES TO ANCHOR NEAR
US. WE RECOGNIZE HER AS THE RETIREMENT HOME OF JIM
EMMET. IT WAS ONE OF EMMET'S "GADGETS AND GILHICKIES"
COLUMNS IN YACHTING MAGAZINE THAT INSPIRED THE INSTAL-
LATION OF *SEA WIND'S* WOOD STOVE, SO NECESSARY TO OUR
ENJOYMENT OF THIS WINTER CRUISING. WE NOTE THAT
CHINOOK SPORTS HER OWN CHARLIE NOBLE.

WE TAKE A LIE-ABOUT,
READING UP ON HENRY
PLUMMER'S ADVENTUROUS
PASSAGE IN THE OCEAN
FROM BEAUFORT TO THE
CAPE FEAR RIVER. IT
WAS DECEMBER. THE
WEATHER BEGAN TO

DETERIORATE AND THEY TRIED TO COME IN
THE NEW RIVER INLET. THE RESULT
WAS A BUSTED UP LAUNCH AND A
HOLED *MASCOT.* THE SURF
POUNDED THEM OVER THE
BAR WHERE THEY LAY IN A
NARROW GUT INSIDE A STRIP
OF BEACH WHILE A SIZZLING NORTHER

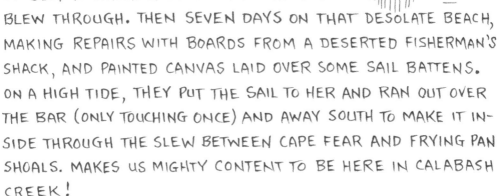

"BILGED"
(AFTER HENRY
PLUMMER)

BLEW THROUGH. THEN SEVEN DAYS ON THAT DESOLATE BEACH,
MAKING REPAIRS WITH BOARDS FROM A DESERTED FISHERMAN'S
SHACK, AND PAINTED CANVAS LAID OVER SOME SAIL BATTENS.
ON A HIGH TIDE, THEY PUT THE SAIL TO HER AND RAN OUT OVER
THE BAR (ONLY TOUCHING ONCE) AND AWAY SOUTH TO MAKE IT IN-
SIDE THROUGH THE SLEW BETWEEN CAPE FEAR AND FRYING PAN
SHOALS. MAKES US MIGHTY CONTENT TO BE HERE IN CALABASH
CREEK!

AKENED AT FIVE A.M. BY THUNDER, LIGHTNING AND
WIND. MIGHT AS WELL HAVE COFFEE AND LET THE DAY COME ON.
BAKE UP SOME BRAN MUFFINS. FINALLY, GREY DAY OR NO, WIND
N.W., BUNDLE UP, AND HIE AWAY THROUGH PINE ISLAND CUT. WE
PUT THE MAIN TO HER TO HELP US ALONG, EVEN THOUGH THE WIND
IS OFTEN BLANKETED BY HIGH BANKS. THE CUT'S A PLACE TO
PAY ATTENTION. IT'S VERY NARROW AT TIMES WITH LEDGES
MAKING OUT FROM BOTH SIDES; A LOT OF DEBRIS IN THE WATER.
SEA WIND HITS A DEADHEAD WITH A SOLID THUMP, BUT WITH-
OUT DAMAGE. THEN A CLOSE ENCOUNTER
WITH A TUG AND BARGE.

DITTO THE CRUISE SHIP *CHARLESTON*, WHICH IN THE DISTANCE APPEARS TO FILL THE ENTIRE CHANNEL.

Lots of shore development GOING ON. A COUPLE OF GOLF COURSES SURROUND US - ONE IS SPLIT BY OUR WATERWAY. CABLE CARS CARRY THE GOLFERS OVERHEAD. IT'S A RELIEF TO JOIN THE **Waccamaw River**, IN ITS NATURAL WATERCOURSE. THIS IS FRESH WATER. MOSS-DRAPED CYPRESS TREES APPEAR. BANKS ARE HEAVILY WOODED AND THE WATER'S DEEP TO THE EDGES. THE WACCAMAW RIVER IS ONE OF THE MOST ATTRACTIVE SECTIONS OF THE INTRACOASTAL, WITH MANY NAVIGABLE DEEP-WATER CREEKS FEEDING IT.

BELOW ENTERPRISE LANDING, OPPOSITE GREEN #29, IS A LOOP WHERE WE DROP THE HOOK. AT THIS TIME OF YEAR, THE TONES ARE MUTED; GREY TREE TRUNKS WITH SPANISH MOSS DRIFTING DOWN.

THE CYPRESS ARE ON LITTLE ISLANDS OF THEIR OWN WITH TEA-COLORED WATER SPREADING BETWEEN.

*F*ROST ON DECK COME MORNING, BUT THE SUN WILL WARM THINGS UP FOR A SHORE EXCURSION: A FEW MILES DOWN IS WACHESAW LANDING AND A MARINA WHERE WE CAN PUT OUR FOLDING BIKES ASHORE. WE WANT TO RIDE TO **Brookgreen Gardens**, A REMARKABLE STATE-OWNED OPEN-AIR SCULPTURE MUSEUM. A MILE OR SO BEYOND THE LANDING IS BROOKGREEN CREEK WHICH ONCE GAVE WATERBORNE VISITORS ACCESS TO THE GARDENS; NOW CHAINED OFF AND CLOSED TO BOATS DUE TO VANDALISM SOME YEARS AGO.

*A*RCHER MILTON HUNTINGTON OWNED THIS FORMER PLANTA-TION, WHICH COVERS SOME 4,400 ACRES. THERE'S NOTHING LEFT OF THE PLANTATION HOUSE, BUT THE AVENUE OF HUGE, GNARLED LIVE OAKS DRIPPING WITH SPANISH MOSS, AND THE BOXWOOD HEDGES ARE FROM THOSE DAYS. THERE'S OUT-STANDING LANDSCAPING, FORMAL GARDENS, FOUNTAINS AND POOLS, FLOWERS IN SEASON,

AND AN EXTENSIVE COLLECTION OF AMERICAN STATUARY AND SCULPTURE IN MAGNIFICENT OUTDOOR SETTINGS:

- 41 -

MARBLES AND BRONZES, FROM SMALL TO MONU-
MENTAL, MANY THE WORK OF THE OWNER'S WIFE,
SCULPTRESS ANNA HYATT HUNTINGTON. THERE'S
EVEN AN AREA SET ASIDE FOR A GAME SANC-
TUARY. WELL WORTH THE AFTERNOON WE SPENT
TAKING IT ALL IN.

*F*OR THE NIGHT, WE ANCHOR ACROSS THE
RIVER FROM THE MARINA IN COW HOUSE CREEK.
THE FULL MOON RISES. AN OWL SHOWS IN

THE BRANCHES
AGAINST ITS
LIGHT.

A LAZY
BREAKFAST
WAITING FOR
A FAIR TIDE TO
GEORGETOWN. THEN THE PLEASURE OF A SAIL DOWN THE
WACCAMAW TO THE POINT WHERE IT DEBOUCHES INTO WINYAH
BAY. GEORGETOWN IS A TERMINUS FOR RIVER TRADE AT THE HEAD
OF WINYAH BAY, THE CONFLUENCE OF THE SAMPIT, BLACK, WACCA-
MAW, AND PEEDEE RIVERS. IT WAS LAID OUT IN 1721 AND NAMED
FOR THE THEN PRINCE OF WALES, GEORGE II. THE LITTLE SEAPORT
ONCE DEALT IN NAVAL STORES, RICE, AND INDIGO. (NAVAL STORES:
PITCH, TAR, RESIN, FLAX, CORDAGE, MASTS, AND TIMBER USED IN
BUILDING AND MAINTAINING WOODEN SAILING SHIPS.) THE INDIGO
TRADE PERISHED WITH THE REVOLUTION AND RICE GROWING WAS
ABANDONED SOON AFTER. NOW THEY HAVE STEEL AND KRAFT
PAPER MILLS, WHOSE PALL HANGS OVER THE CITY.

SEA WIND ANCHORS JUST OFF THE ISLAND ACROSS FROM

THE TOWN DOCKS.
A LOT OF SHRIMPERS
IN PORT. AT THE
GULF DOCK WE
FILL A JERRY CAN
WITH GAS. UP TOWN

GEORGETOWN

WE SHOP AND SEARCH OUT A BIT OF PRINTER'S INK AT THE
LOCAL NEWSPAPER OFFICE, SO WE CAN PRINT UP A CHRIST-
MAS CARD FROM THE WOOD BLOCK THE MATE'S BEEN CARVING.

*T*HE OVERNIGHT DEW HAS TURNED TO ICE ON DECK.
GEORGETOWN ISN'T VERY APPEALING TO US AND WE LEAVE THE
SMOG WITH HARDLY A BACKWARDS GLANCE.* DOWN WINYAH
BAY THE MARKERS TEMPORARILY READ FROM
SEAWARD. SOON WE'RE IN CLOSE QUARTERS
AFTER TURNING SHARPLY TO STARBOARD TO
ENTER THE ESTHERVILLE-MINIM CREEK CANAL.
VAST MARSHES STRETCH AWAY ON EITHER SIDE.
INDIAN PUDDING IS SIMMERING ON THE WOOD
STOVE AS WE GO.

*W*E ANCHOR EARLY, IN THE NORTH
SANTEE RIVER TO THE WEST OF THE WATERWAY.
MR. GRAY SEASCOUT HAS A PROBLEM AND
THE TIME HAS COME FOR THE SKIPPER
TO SEARCH IT OUT. THE CULPRIT TURNS
OUT TO BE RUST SCALE IN AN ELBOW OF

---

* GEORGETOWN, LIKE MANY WATERWAY COMMUNITIES, HAS RECENTLY REVITAL-
IZED ITS HISTORIC DISTRICT AND DOWNTOWN BUSINESS AREA. A TRAM
TOUR TAKES YOU PAST PRE-REVOLUTIONARY AND ANTEBELLUM HOMES.
THE CITY'S BUILT A FLOATING DINGHY DOCK, PART OF A HARBORWALK
THAT HAS TWO WATERFRONT PARKS WITH BRICK SIDEWALKS AND GASLIGHTS.

THE COOLING SYSTEM, CAUSING ERRATIC ENGINE HEATING. I C W CRUISING DEMANDS A RELIABLE MOTOR, ESPECIALLY SINCE OUR NEXT EXCURSION AWAY FROM THE WATERWAY WILL BE INTO UNMARKED, LITTLE USED CHANNELS. NO TIME TO HAVE A SICK ENGINE.

ASHORE HERE ARE A NUMBER OF DEAD TREES ALONG THE EDGE OF THE SWAMP. WE WITNESS AN UNUSUAL SCENE: A BALD EAGLE WITH HIS KILL ON ONE LIMB, WHILE LOWER DOWN IN A CROTCH OF THE SAME TREE, A RACCOON CALMLY CLEANS HIMSELF AND THEN ROLLS INTO A BALL TO HAVE A NAP.

OL' BLACK CAT WAKES US AT FIVE TIPPING OVER THE KINDLING BUCKET; CLIMBS ON THE BUNKS AND POKES AT THE COVERS. IT APPEARS WE ARE SUPPOSED TO GET UP EARLY. THEN IT'S DOWN THROUGH THE CUTS AND RIVERS. STREAMS ENTER FROM DIFFERENT DIRECTIONS, AFFECTING TIDAL CURRENTS IN MYSTERIOUS WAYS.

BELOW McCLELLANVILLE (NEAR MILE 440) WE COME UPON A LARGE DREDGE, STRADDLING THE CHANNEL. A TRAWLER IS HARD AGROUND ON THE WEST SIDE OF THE CUT. SHE'S SWUNG TOO WIDE IN PASSING THE DREDGE AND THE TIDE HAS LEFT HER HIGH AND DRY UNTIL IT RETURNS. WE THREAD THROUGH THE FLAGGED STAKES TO SCRAPE BY, DRAGGING MUD, AND SOON AFTER FOLLOW PRICE CREEK OUT OF THE INTRACOASTAL AS FAR AS BULL NARROWS. HERE WE DROP THE HOOK.

BULL ISLAND

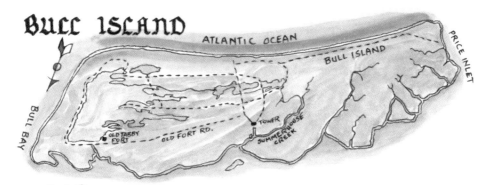

ATLANTIC OCEAN

BULL ISLAND

PRICE INLET

BULL BAY

OLD TABBY FORT

OLD FORT RD.

TOWER

SUMMERHOUSE CREEK

WE'RE ON THE VERGE OF A TRULY SPORTING PROPOSITION. WE HAVE OUR EYE ON BULL ISLAND, PART OF THE CAPE ROMAIN WILDLIFE REFUGE. BULL ISLAND CONTAINS ENORMOUS FRESH WATER PONDS, THE RESIDUE OF A ONCE FLOURISHING RICE CULTURE. THE PONDS, NOW DECAYED TO FRESHWATER MARSHES, WERE CREATED WITH EMBANKMENTS AND CAUSEWAYS (SLAVE LABOR) TO TRAP AND RETAIN FRESH WATER. THIS RESOURCE, SO UNUSUAL FOR A BARRIER ISLAND, MAKES BULL ISLAND A SPECTACULAR MIX OF SALT MARSH, TIDAL CREEKS, FRESH WATER MARSHES AND SWAMPS, FOREST, DUNE, AND OCEAN-BEACH ECOLOGY. THE PONDS SERVE AS BREEDING, NESTING, AND WINTERING HABITAT FOR WATERFOWL – AND HARBOR A LARGE POPULATION OF ALLIGATORS. THE OCEAN BEACHES, IN SEASON, ARE A REPOSITORY FOR THE EGGS OF THE LOGGERHEAD TURTLE.*

---

* SINCE OUR VISIT, THIS PART OF THE COAST HAS BEEN DEVASTATED BY AN EXTRAORDINARY HURRICANE, DRAMATICALLY CHANGING THE ISLAND, ITS ECOLOGY, AND THE CHANNELS LEADING TO IT.

BABY LOGGERHEAD

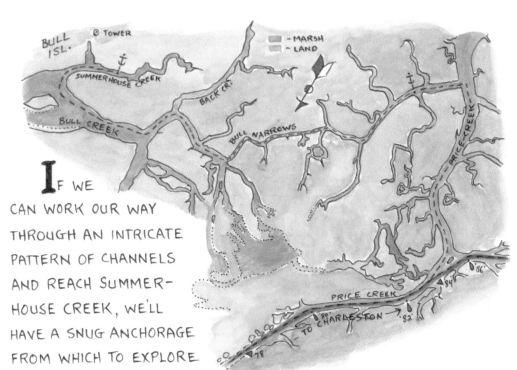

IF WE CAN WORK OUR WAY THROUGH AN INTRICATE PATTERN OF CHANNELS AND REACH SUMMER-HOUSE CREEK, WE'LL HAVE A SNUG ANCHORAGE FROM WHICH TO EXPLORE THIS NATURALISTS' PARADISE. NOT THIS AFTERNOON, HOWEVER. A LIGHT RAIN IS FALLING AND SO IS THE TIDE. WE MUST MAKE OUR ATTEMPT ON A RISING TIDE. THE INVISIBLE CLAPPER RAILS (MARSH HENS) ARE CACKLING AWAY. ALONG THE SHORE ARE OYSTERS. HOW SHALL WE FIX THEM TONIGHT? SCALLOPED!

THE RAIN MOVES AWAY OVERNIGHT, AND THE RISING TIDE SHOWS US BULL ISLAND CLEAR ABOVE THE GRASSES. SKIMMERS ARE FISHING. WE WORK THROUGH BULL NARROWS COUNTING THE SMALL FEEDER STREAMS TO KEEP TRACK OF WHERE WE ARE, THEN INTO BULL CREEK AND CAREFULLY AROUND THE SHOAL (AFTER THE SKIPPER ANCHORS *SEA WIND* TO

SOUND AHEAD IN THE DINGHY) AND INTO SUMMERHOUSE CREEK. WE
ANCHOR BEYOND THE REFUGE DOCKS. NICE COVERED DOCKS FOR
THE USE OF THE REFUGE
PERSONNEL. THEY'RE
PLASTERED WITH SIGNS
"DANGER, KEEP OFF", "NO
TRESPASSING", "NO DOCKING".
THIS POLICY IS APPARENTLY
INTENDED TO PROTECT AGAINST
LITIGATION. CONSEQUENTLY, OUR
ONLY RECOURSE IS TO PULL THE DINGHY
UP ON A MUDDY SHORE. WITH THE FIVE-FOOT
TIDAL RANGE HERE, THAT MEANS MUD EITHER COMING
OR GOING. AND STICKY MUD IT IS, TOO.

In KEEPING WITH THE DEPARTMENT
OF FISHERIES AND WILDLIFE POLICY, PARTS
OF THE REFUGE ARE PERIODICALLY OPEN TO
PUBLIC BOW HUNTING IF THE STATUS OF THE
SPECIES POPULATION WARRANTS IT.
THIS YEAR WE FIND DEER HUNTERS
CAMPED ASHORE. IT'S THEIR LAST DAY, WE'RE
GRATIFIED TO LEARN. WALKING THE ISLAND ON TIPTOE EXPECTING
AN ARROW THROUGH YOUR CAP AT ANY MINUTE CRAMPS OUR STYLE.

Paths TAKE US TO BOTH ENDS OF THE ISLAND AND ACROSS THE
PONDS TO THE OCEAN BEACH. OVER A PERIOD OF DAYS WE CARRY
LUNCHES AND BINOCULARS ASHORE AND
HIKE THE WHOLE ISLAND. THERE
ARE MAGNIFICENT LIVE OAKS,
MAGNOLIAS, PINES, PALMETTOS,
AND MYRTLES.

Our sightings: the unique large black fox squirrel with white nose and ear tips, raccoon, deer, alligators (including great big ones and wee yellow-banded ones), canvasback, blue winged teal, crows, bufflehead, kingfishers, ibises, egret, mallard, wood ducks, cardinals, pileated woodpeckers, greater yellowlegs, grackle, coots, limpkins, marsh hens, red-winged blackbirds, great blue herons, green herons, sandpipers, cormorants, pelicans, marsh hawks,

WOOD DUCK

GREEN HERON

LIMPKIN

COOT

gulls, flicker, scoter, skimmers, terns, and a flight of eleven whistling swans overhead at noon one day.

GULL

We take dinghy trips up summer-house creek, with Billy along as bow watch, and out into Bull Bay past its salt marshes and mud flats. Each night, we have the sound of the marsh hens "tick, ticking" nearby in the grasses.

OPENING
OYSTERS

SUNSET IN SUMMERHOUSE CREEK
SCRUBBING OYSTERS FROM THE DINK

ONE NIGHT, WIND AND RAIN. A SWELL WORKS IN FROM THE OCEAN. *SEA WIND* GOES TURN AND TURN AND TURN ABOUT IN THE TIDEWAY, HEELING TO THE GUSTS. WITH WIND AND TIDE OPPOSED, THE DINGHY THUMPS THE TRANSOM UNTIL THE SKIPPER TIES IT ALONGSIDE IN THE GREY DAWN, WHICH SHOWS US LOW, DARK, DRIVING SCUD ALOFT. THE VHF REPORTS WIND N.E. 40 KNOTS AT FRYING PAN SHOALS. LATER WE WALK THE WIDE, BEAUTIFUL OCEAN BEACH, DECORATED WITH A FRESH STORM WRACK. HAVING LEARNED FROM THE OFFICIALS THAT VISITORS ARE WELCOME TO COLLECT SHELLS FROM THE BEACH, WE GATHER A FEW SOUVENIRS: WHELKS, RAZORS, TUNS, PENS, TELLINS, MOONSHELLS, QUAHOGS, AND COCKLES. THE LARGE COCKLES FIND AN IMMEDIATE PRACTICAL USE; BACK ABOARD WE STUFF THEM WITH CHOPPED CLAMS, OYSTERS, AND VIRGINIA HAM

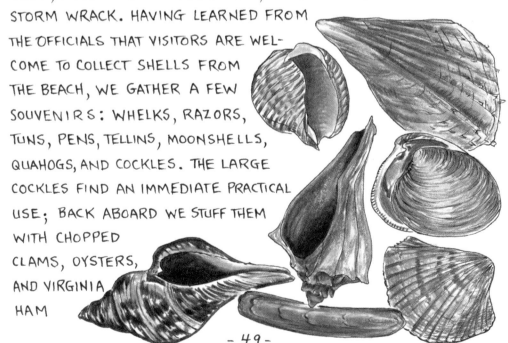

MIXED WITH BREAD CRUMBS, ONION, EGG, AND PARSLEY. BAKED WITH A PIECE OF BACON ON TOP. SERVED WITH A BOTTLE OF CHAMPAGNE TO CELEBRATE BULL ISLAND DAYS.

ONE SUNNY MORNING A FAIR WIND WHISPERS IT'S TIME TO LEAVE. THE SKIPPER SETS *SEA WIND'S* SKYRAKER TO CATCH THE BREEZE ABOVE THE MARSHES, AND WE WIND THIS WAY AND THAT, BACK THROUGH BULL

NARROWS TO PRICE CREEK, THE ICW, AND SOUTH AGAIN. A SUPERIOR SAIL TO CHARLESTON ENSUES, WITH ONLY ONE FRAUGHT MOMENT AT THE BEN SAWYER MEMORIAL SWING BRIDGE WITH ITS TIMED OPENINGS. OUR APPROACH COINCIDES WITH THE NORTH-

BOUND PASSAGE OF A DREDGE AND STRINGOUT (ASSOCIATED PIPES AND BARGES), PLUS A WHOLE FLEET OF TUGS (BIG AND LITTLE) RUNNING AROUND THE EDGES TO PUSH AND PULL. ON TENTER-

HOOKS OURSELVES IN THE LIMITED

SPACE, IN AN EASILY-HANDLED YACHT, WE CAN ONLY SALUTE THE SKILL OF THE DREDGE SKIPPER AS WE SLIP PAST HIS CUMBERSOME LINEUP

AND INTO CHARLESTON HARBOR.

CHARLESTON

(CHARLES TOWNE, AFTER
ENGLAND'S KING CHARLES II)
DATES FROM THE 1670'S.
STRATEGIC LOCATION, BETWEEN
THE COOPER AND ASHLEY RIVERS,
SOON MADE IT A CENTER OF COMMERCE.
RICH PLANTATION COMMUNITIES DEVELOPED
ALONG THE RIVERS AND CREEKS, WHICH WERE
THE HIGHWAYS OF THE SURROUNDING LOW COUNTRY.

WE BECOME MARINA RESIDENTS FOR A WEEK; THE
FLOATING DOCKS ALLOW US TO LAUNCH OUR
BIKES AND ROAM THE PICTURESQUE
STREETS TO STEEP OUR-
SELVES IN CHARLESTON'S
CULTURE. HOT SHOWERS
AND A COMPLIMENTARY
NEWSPAPER EVERY
MORNING ARE WELCOME
LUXURIES.

FOR A YACHT TRAVELING NORTH WITH THE
SPRING, CHARLESTON'S SPOLETO FESTIVAL OFFERS AN
EXCITING WEEK OF CONCERTS, ART, AND LIVE PERFOR-
MANCES SET IN PARKS,
CHURCHES, AND OTHER
HISTORICAL BUILDINGS.

OUR MAIL CATCHES UP
WITH US HERE, AS DOES
CHRISTMAS.

HOMEMADE CHRISTMAS CARD

Sea Islands — SEA WIND IS NOW ON THE

NORTHERN THRESHOLD OF THE SEA ISLANDS
WHICH LIE LOW OFF THE COASTS OF SOUTH
CAROLINA, GEORGIA, AND FLORIDA (BE-
TWEEN THE SANTEE AND ST. JOHNS
RIVERS). THEY'RE ALL WITHIN EASY
REACH OF ANYONE RUNNING
THE INTRACOASTAL. THEIR RICH HISTORIES ARE VARIED. OFTEN,
THEY WERE THE FIRST PLACES OF SETTLEMENT FOR PEOPLE
COMING FROM EUROPE. SOME WERE CLAIMED AND SETTLED
BY THE SPANISH (WHO WERE WELL ENSCONSED IN FLORIDA)
UNTIL DRIVEN OFF BY THE BRITISH. THE ISLANDS WERE
ORIGINALLY PART OF LARGE LAND GRANTS THE ENGLISH CROWN
GAVE TO FAVORED PATRONS. SOME BECAME PRIVATE LITTLE
KINGDOMS OF THE WEALTHY. OSSABAW, SAPELLO, AND ST.
CATHERINES WERE AWARDED TO MARY MUSGROVE (HALF-BREED
INTERPRETER FOR GENERAL JAMES OGLETHORP). SHE WAS
MARRIED TO ONE THOMAS BOSOMWORTH, A
PRIEST OF THE CHURCH OF ENGLAND, WHO IN-
DUCED MARY TO DECLARE HERSELF EMPRESS OF
THE CREEK INDIANS AND AS SUCH, TO DEMAND HER
RIGHTS IN THE FORM OF LAND. AFTER YEARS OF IN-
TRIGUE, SHE RECEIVED A GIFT OF THE THREE ISLANDS.
SUBSEQUENTLY THEY PASSED ALONG TO VARIOUS
PURCHASERS, BUT THE BOSOMWORTHS RETIRED TO
AND LEFT THEIR BONES ON ST. CATHERINES.
RICE AND COTTON PLANTATIONS WERE ES-
TABLISHED, ESPECIALLY ON THE SOUTH CAROLINA
ISLANDS OF ST. HELENA AND PORT ROYAL WHERE
THE LONG STAPLE SEA ISLAND COTTON WAS

-52-

DEVELOPED. AFTER THE CIVIL WAR, ABANDONED PLANTATIONS WERE CONFISCATED AND THE LAND GIVEN TO FREED SLAVES. A FEW WOUND UP IN PRIVATE HANDS — SAPELO, JEKYLL, AND CUMBERLAND. A NUMBER ARE NOW WILDLIFE REFUGES AND NATIONAL PARKS. SOME ARE RESORTS.

SEA WIND'S WAY NOW WENDS ACROSS WIDE RIVER MOUTHS, THROUGH SOUNDS AND BEHIND (SOMETIMES ACROSS) COASTAL INLETS WITH OCCASIONAL GLIMPSES OF THE OCEAN. WE'RE FOLLOWING NATURAL WATERWAYS WHICH, ON THE CHART, RESEMBLE A RANDOM SCRAWL CURVING THIS WAY AND THAT. THERE'S NO BETTER DESCRIPTION FOR THIS COUNTRY THAN HENRY PLUMMER'S, WRITTEN IN 1912 : "AM NOT GOING TO WRITE DAILY LOG OF THIS TIME FOR IT WOULD BE TOO TEDIOUS READING, BUT IT WAS BY NO MEANS TEDIOUS LIVING. WE BECAME PART AND PARCEL OF THE SWAMP AND MARSH. WE WERE OF IT, IN IT, AND PASSED THROUGH IT LIKE A MUSKRAT OR MINK, LIKE A SNIPE OR PLOVER. THE TIDE; ITS SET, SPEED, AND TURNING. THE WIND; ITS STRENGTH AND DIRECTION. THESE WERE WHAT COUNTED AND ON THEM WE EITHER HALTED OR WENT ON. THE RIPPLE OF THE TIDE AT EVERY BEND, THE LINE OF FOAM BUBBLES ON EVERY REACH WAS A MATTER OF CONSTANT INTEREST AND STUDY. SUCH DAYS ARE NOT FOR EITHER RICH OR POOR, FOR THOSE IGNORANT OR WISE, BUT FOR THOSE ONLY WHO CAN CAST THEMSELVES BODILY INTO NATURE AND BE ABSORBED BY IT. I DON'T WONDER BIG LAUNCH OWNERS AND HOUSEBOAT OWNERS ALWAYS SEND THEIR BOATS SOUTH UNDER CHARGE OF THE CREW. THERE COULD BE NOTHING MORE DREARY THAN JUST A-SETTING STILL AND BEING TAKEN THROUGH THESE TWISTING RIVERS THAT LEAD FOR MILES AND MILES THROUGH THE NEVER ENDING RICE MARSHES."

THE LANDSCAPE IS PREDOMINENTLY MARSH, SOMETIMES BACKED WITH WOODS, OR HAMMOCKS OF VEGETATION AND TREES.

Hammocks:

ISOLATED STANDS OF TREES (OAKS, EVERGREENS, AND PALMETTOS) WITH DENSE UNDERGROWTH, OFTEN SOMEWHAT HIGHER THAN THE SURROUNDING MARSH; THE SOIL RICHER WITH HUMUS THAN THE FLATWOODS OR PINELANDS. THEY MAY HAVE BEEN FORMED FROM ANCIENT DUNE RIDGES, DETRITUS BUILT UP AT THE MEETING PLACES OF SMALL CREEKS, OR AN OLD INDIAN MOUND. THEY PROVIDE A REFUGE FOR MANY BIRDS AND SMALL MAMMALS. COMPLETE MICROCOSMS. FOR *SEA WIND*, HAMMOCKS ARE OF SPECIAL INTEREST. THEIR TREES CAN SHELTER AN ANCHORAGE (FOR DEEP WATER OFTEN RUNS CLOSE TO THESE ISLETS IN THE MARSH); THEIR ANIMAL AND BIRD LIFE PROVIDES MORE EXERCISE FOR THE BINOCULARS; AND THEIR HARD BEACHES ARE A WELCOME OPPORTUNITY TO STRETCH OUR LEGS AND PERHAPS REPLENISH OUR SUPPLY OF DRIFTWOOD FOR THE CABIN STOVE.

COMING AWAY FROM CHARLESTON, WE TICK OFF INTRIGUING NAMES AS WE PASS: WAPPOO CREEK, STONO RIVER, WADMALAW RIVER, DAWHO RIVER, TOOGOODOO CREEK, ASHEPOO RIVER. WE PAY ATTENTION TO RANGES AND DAYMARKS. THERE'S LOTS OF SHOALING HEREABOUTS. AN ANCHORAGE IS PICKED OUT IN ROCK CREEK, BETWEEN BEET AND HUTCHINSON ISLANDS, WELL OUT OF THE WATERWAY.

ASHEPOO RIVER

ASHEPOO COOSAW CUTOFF

HUTCHINSON ISL.

170'

172'

173'

BM

ROCK CR.

176'

177'

BEET ISL.

ASHEPOO COOSAW CUTOFF

181'

	— WATER
	— MARSH
	— LAND

WE CALL THIS OUR
OASIS ANCHORAGE;
THE HAMMOCK
WITH ITS CABBAGE
PALMETTOS RECALLS
THE DESERT IMAGE.

THERE'S AN ALLIGATOR
NEAR THE SHORE GIVING
US THE EYE. FOR THE FIRST TIME IN A LONG WHILE HAVE TO
SCREEN UP AGAINST MOSQUITOS AND SAND FLIES. TWO SAILBOATS
COME TO JOIN US, ONE SETTLES CLOSE ENOUGH TO RAFT UP. IT'S
A CURIOUS PHENOMENON — THIS HERDING INSTINCT. A QUARTER
MILE OF SHORE WITH DEEP WATER OFFERS, BUT THE
NEWCOMERS MUST HUDDLE NEXT TO THE
FIRST COMER. WE SIT IN THE COCKPIT AFTER DINNER AND LISTEN
TO THE BLOWING AND SNORTING OF PORPOISES AROUND US IN THE DARK.

OUR LITTLE ALLIGATOR IS
STILL VISIBLE WHEN WE LEAVE
AT FIRST LIGHT. WE HAVE
A GREAT SAIL ALL THE
WAY TO **BEAUFORT**
(BEWFORT); DOWN
THE COOSAW RIVER AND INTO BRICKYARD CREEK (HEADWATERS
OF THE BEAUFORT RIVER). A FEW SHRIMPERS ARE OUT
DRAGGING IN ST. HELENA SOUND,
TAKING ADVANTAGE OF THE
GOOD WEATHER. FURL
ALL AT THE LADIES IS-
LAND BRIDGE, AND BE-
YOND THE DOWNTOWN

A HARD LIFE FOR CATS!

MARINA, SET THE ANCHOR. AFTER LUNCH WE WALK THROUGH
THE ATTRACTIVE WATERFRONT PARK, DOWN TOWN, SIDE STREETS
WITH THEIR ELEGANT OLD HOMES AND THE ROAD ON THE HIGH
BLUFF ALONG THE RIVER, WITH YET MORE OLD GRACIOUS HOUSES,
MANY OF WHICH HAVE BEEN RESTORED.

COMES GREY AND COLD. THE PREDICTION IS "SHOWERS", BUT
THE WIND IS FAIR. *SEA WIND* SAILS OFF THE HOOK, DOWN THE
BEAUFORT RIVER INTO PORT ROYAL SOUND. MANY POTENTIAL AN-
CHORAGES IF BAD WEATHER FORCES A STOP. IT'S SPITTING LIGHTLY

AND GETTING COLDER. THE RED
WOOL BLANKET COMES OUT TO
WRAP AROUND THE HELMSMAN'S
LEGS. WE GIVE WELL-DE-
VELOPED HILTON HEAD ISLAND
THE BY; THIS ISN'T THE RIGHT
DAY TO EXPLORE THIS LARGEST
OF THE SOUTHERN BARRIER
ISLANDS. WE MAKE GOOD
TIME DOWN CALIBOGUE
SOUND, THE MATE BELOW STOKING THE FIRE AND BAKING IRISH
SODA BREAD. *SEA WIND* ENTERS THE COOPER RIVER, JIBES
THROUGH RAMSHORN CREEK, AND ROUNDS UP TO ANCHOR IN THE
NEW RIVER, JUST AS THE WIND INCREASES AND IT SETTLES DOWN
TO A STEADY RAIN. IT'S A FINE FEELING TO RELAX IN THE WARM
CABIN WITH A GOOD RUN (ALL UNDER SAIL) BEHIND US. THIS IS A
MARSH ANCHORAGE. OFF TO THE EAST IS DAUFUSKIE ISLAND, ANOTHER
PLACE WITH LOTS OF DEVELOPMENT GOING ON, A LA HILTON HEAD.

On CHILLY MORNINGS, IT'S HARD
TO LEAVE THE WARM BUNK. THE SKIPPER
STARTS UP FIRES AND DISCUSSES POSSIBILITIES
WITH THE CAT. IT'S A PEACH OF A DAY, WITH
THE SKY WASHED CLEAR BLUE. MUSTN'T
LIE ABED. THERE'S ANOTHER FAIR WIND
WAITING SO IT'S **Georgia** OR BUST. WE'VE
BEEN READING UP ON SAVANNAH HOPING WE'D
HAVE A CHANCE TO VISIT THIS VERY SOUTHERN
OLD CITY. SAVANNAH'S WATERFRONT IS A
POTENTIALLY DANGEROUS PLACE FOR A
YACHT. EIGHT MILES UPSTREAM FROM THE I C W, THE NINE FOOT
TIDES MAKE DOCKING DIFFICULT IN THE FIERCE CURRENTS AND
THERE'S HEAVY COMMERCIAL TRAFFIC. WE DECIDE TO APPROACH IT
FROM ANOTHER DIRECTION.

We CROSS THE SWIFTLY FLOWING SAVANNAH RIVER UNDER
MAIN AND JIB. ON V H F CHANNEL 13 WE TALK OPEN THE CAUSTON
BLUFF BRIDGE AND THE THUNDERBOLT BRIDGE ON THE WILMINGTON
RIVER — WINDING, WINDING, TO PRETTY *Isle of Hope* ON A BLUFF HIGH
ABOVE A BEND IN THE RIVER, WHICH WILL GIVE US ACCESS TO
SAVANNAH. HERE WE COME TO REST IN THE SPOT DENOTED
ON THE CHART "ANCHORING AREA". THIS NOTATION
IS ESPECIALLY WELCOME TO WATER TRAVEL-
LERS. IT MEANS THE TOWN OR CITY HAS SET
ASIDE A PLACE FOR THIS PURPOSE AND IS
HAPPY TO HAVE YOU VISIT. WE FIND THE
MARINA FRIENDLY AND FOR A PITTANCE
WE (AND THE BIKES) GAIN ACCESS ASHORE
TO GET THE FEEL OF THE PLACE. AN ES-
PECIALLY LOVELY WATERFRONT WITH

SPACIOUS OLD HOMES AND TREES. WE RIDE TO WORMSLOE PLANTA-
TION TO FIND
AN UNBELIEV-
ABLE AVENUE
OF OLD OAKS
FORMING
AN ARCHWAY
ABOUT A
MILE LONG
LEADING TO
A SMALL

MUSEUM, WHICH GIVES THE HISTORY OF GEORGIA AND THIS EX-
PLANTATION. BUILT BY ONE NOBLE JONES. THE MANSION'S STILL
STANDING; BUT OCCUPIED BY JONES' DESCENDENTS, AND THEREFORE
NOT AVAILABLE FOR VIEWING.

To Savannah BY BUS THE NEXT DAY. THE CITY WAS LAID OUT IN
ENGLAND ON A SYMMETRICAL PLAT LEAVING NUMEROUS SQUARES FOR
PUBLIC PARKS. THE STATE OF GEORGIA (NAMED FOR GEORGE II) WAS THE
LAST OF THE 13 ORIGINAL COLONIES TO BE FOUNDED AND WAS FORMED AS
A BUFFER BETWEEN THE SPANISH (IN FLORIDA), THE FRENCH (IN LOUISIANA),
AND THE CAROLINAS. CREATED BY A GROUP OF BRITISH PHILANTHROPISTS WHO
OBTAINED A GRANT OF LAND BETWEEN THE ALTAMAHA AND SAVANNAH
RIVERS. THEY WANTED A REFUGE FOR THE PERSECUTED PROTESTANT SECTS
AND UNFORTUNATE BUT WORTHY INDIGENT CLASSES IN ENGLAND. GENERAL
JAMES OGLETHORPE BROUGHT 100 SETTLERS OUT IN 1733 AND ESTABLISHED
THIS TOWN. IDEALISM (SLAVERY WAS PROHIBITED, AS WAS ALCOHOL AND
THERE WERE SEVERE RESTRICTIONS ON LAND TENURE) INADVERTENTLY RE-
TARDED GEORGIA'S GROWTH. IT WAS SUCCESSFUL AS A BULWARK AGAINST
THE SPANISH AND THE FRENCH, BUT ECONOMICALLY AND PHILANTHROPI-
CALLY A FAILURE. INDUSTRIES PLANNED DIDN'T THRIVE — THE PLANTERS

COULDN'T GET ANY LABOR; COULDN'T TRADE LUMBER FOR RUM.
GRADUALLY THE IDEAL WAS CORRUPTED BY ECONOMIC PRAGMATISM
AND IN 1753 WHEN THE CHARTER EXPIRED, THE CROWN TOOK OVER.

WE EXPLORE THE HISTORIC DOWNTOWN AND ITS OLD BUILDINGS,
STOPPING IN ART GALLERIES AND MUSEUMS.
ALWAYS DRAWN TO THE WATERFRONT, WE
SPEND TIME ON RIVER ST. : FACTORS'
WALK, TALL STONE WAREHOUSES BUILT
AGAINST THE FORTY FOOT HIGH BLUFF,
WITH ENTRANCES ON BOTH LEVELS,
COBBLESTONE STREETS, IRON AND
WOODEN BRIDGES, SHOPS, RESTAU-
RANTS GALORE (WHERE WE MUZZLE
INTO OYSTERS AND SHRIMPS).
BACK IN ISLE OF HOPE WE'RE
SWEPT OFF TO A PARTY BY A
LOCAL SAILOR. TYPICAL
WARM SOUTHERN HOSPITALITY
WITH MUCH GOOD FOOD AND TALK.

GUARDING
THE OLD
COTTON
EXCHANGE

THEY INTRODUCE US TO SWEET VIDALIA ONIONS, OF WHICH WE WERE IG-
NORANT. BACK ABOARD VERY LATE TO RUMINATE ON OUR SAVANNAH DAY.

A SLOW, LATE START. WE NOTICE THE MANY QUAINT LITTLE
DOCK SHELTERS (GAZEBOS) LINED ALONG
THIS SHORE. THE SKIPPER CLIMBS
IN THE DINK TO UNSHIP THE OUTBOARD AND
HAND IT UP TO *SEA WIND*. HE'S STARTLED BY
A FACE IN THE WATER BETWEEN BOAT AND DINGHY - WHISKERS
AND BRIGHT EYES. THE RIVER OTTER IS SURPRISED
TOO, ROLLS HIS TAIL AROUND, AND DISAPPEARS
BELOW THE SURFACE. FISHERMEN TELL OF

OTTERS SURFACING ALONGSIDE, STARING AT THEM, ONLY TO SINK
AWAY IN A TRAIL OF BUBBLES.

*T*HEN IT'S AWAY SOUTH FOR US, BOYS.
ROUND THE BEND IN SKIDAWAY NARROWS, WE
COME UPON A BARGE AND TUG AGROUND;
ANOTHER TUG PUSHING AND PULLING TO

GET THEM OFF. *SEA WIND* LUFFS UP, COMES ABOUT AND FOOLS
AROUND UNTIL THEY SORT THEMSELVES OUT, AFTER WHICH WE FIND
OURSELVES BEHIND THE BARGE IN THE NARROWS. HE'S BEING VERY
CAUTIOUS NOW, MOVING AT A SNAIL'S PACE. NOT OFTEN DOES *SEA
WIND* WANT TO PASS COMMERCIAL TRAFFIC; USUALLY
THE OTHER WAY AROUND. WE FINALLY FIND A STRETCH
WHERE WE CAN MOVE AHEAD OF HIM AND
THEN, WITH THE GOOD BREEZE, BOOM AWAY—
FROM BURNSIDE RIVER INTO VERNON
RIVER, FOLLOWING RANGES CAREFULLY.
THROUGH HELL GATE, THE OGEECHEE
RIVER, THE FLORIDA PASSAGE, AND
DOWN THE BEAR RIVER TO
Kilkenny Creek.

WHERE WE GIVE IT UP FOR THE DAY. WE PUTT-PUTT FAR ENOUGH UP
THE CREEK TO LOOK AT QUIET KILKENNY, THEN RETREAT TO
ANCHOR OFF THE MARSH, SUN AND WIND WOOZLED. SKIPPER
TAKES APART A BILGE PUMP AND REPAIRS SAME BY TURNING
OVER A RUBBER FLAPPER VALVE.

$\mathcal{A}$ FARMER'S BREAKFAST WILL START A SAILOR OFF TO PLOW THE WATERS: A COUPLE SLICES OF BACON, CHOPPED AND PARTLY FRIED UP IN THE BLACK IRON SKILLET, SPREAD OVER WITH GRATED RAW POTATOES (A LITTLE ONION TOO), SEASONED UP WITH SALT AND PEPPER, AND COOKED UNTIL CRUSTY BROWN ON THE BOTTOM. LOOSENED AND TURNED (IN ONE PIECE IF POSSIBLE). EGGS ON TOP, SEASONED TO OUR LIKING, COVERED, AND STEAMED ON A LOW FIRE UNTIL THE EGGS ARE SET. SERVED UP WITH A SPRINKLE OF CHOPPED PARSLEY. NOW WE'RE READY TO SAIL AWAY INTO ST. CATHERINES SOUND.

$\mathcal{W}$E FIND IT BLUE AND SUNNY, WITH LIGHT WINDS. IT'S MOTORSAIL TO STEM THE CURRENT. MORE MARSH AND HAMMOCK COUNTRY; THE VIEWS OUT TO THE OCEAN FROM ST.

CATHERINES SOUND, SAPELLO AND DOBOY SOUNDS MISTY AND SHRIMPERS, SHRIMPERS IN THE DISTANCE. GRAND WEATHER TO CROSS THESE WIDE BODIES OF WATER WITH THEIR STRONG CURRENTS, OVER WHICH A GOOD WIND CAN MAKE A DANGEROUS SEA. PASS A SHRIMPER (*TORNADO II*) IN SAPELLO SOUND, WORKING NETS. HE LATER PASSES US.

BEAR RIVER

KILKENNY CREEK

KILKENNY

TORNADO II   TORNADO II

WHEN WE CROSS CRESCENT RIVER, THERE HE IS, AGROUND, BOTTOM PAINT SHOWING, NOSE POKED UP INTO THE MARSH. NOT A SOUL SHOWING ON BOARD. OUR MYSTERY OF THE DAY.

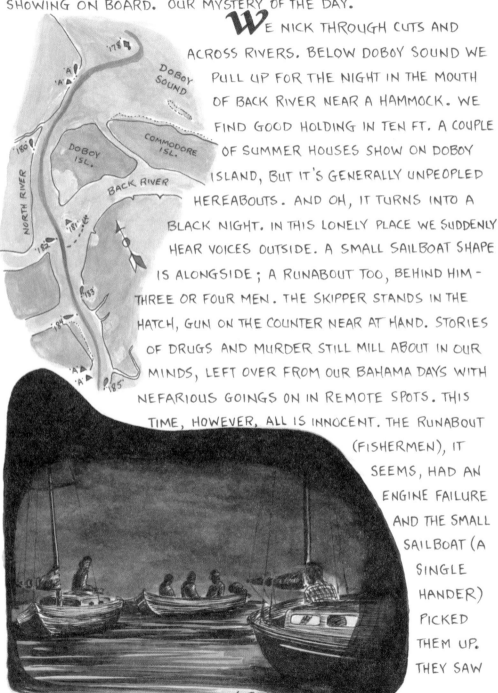

WE NICK THROUGH CUTS AND ACROSS RIVERS. BELOW DOBOY SOUND WE PULL UP FOR THE NIGHT IN THE MOUTH OF BACK RIVER NEAR A HAMMOCK. WE FIND GOOD HOLDING IN TEN FT. A COUPLE OF SUMMER HOUSES SHOW ON DOBOY ISLAND, BUT IT'S GENERALLY UNPEOPLED HEREABOUTS. AND OH, IT TURNS INTO A BLACK NIGHT. IN THIS LONELY PLACE WE SUDDENLY HEAR VOICES OUTSIDE. A SMALL SAILBOAT SHAPE IS ALONGSIDE; A RUNABOUT TOO, BEHIND HIM — THREE OR FOUR MEN. THE SKIPPER STANDS IN THE HATCH, GUN ON THE COUNTER NEAR AT HAND. STORIES OF DRUGS AND MURDER STILL MILL ABOUT IN OUR MINDS, LEFT OVER FROM OUR BAHAMA DAYS WITH NEFARIOUS GOINGS ON IN REMOTE SPOTS. THIS TIME, HOWEVER, ALL IS INNOCENT. THE RUNABOUT (FISHERMEN), IT SEEMS, HAD AN ENGINE FAILURE AND THE SMALL SAILBOAT (A SINGLE HANDER) PICKED THEM UP. THEY SAW

OUR LIGHTS. NEITHER HAS A RADIO. WE CALL THE COAST GUARD
WHICH CALLS THE SHERIFF'S OFFICE IN McINTOSH, WHICH COMES
TO THE RESCUE. SO MUCH FOR THIS NIGHT'S FEARS AND FANCIES.

       Mr. GRAY CARRIES US ON, ACROSS ALTAMAHA SOUND,
THROUGH BUTTERMILK SOUND TO OUR NEXT "DESTINATION", THE
PRETTY FREDERICA RIVER, WHICH RUNS ALONG ST. SIMON'S ISLAND.
ABOUT HALFWAY DOWN THIS ALTERNATE ROUTE IS THE SITE OF A
NATIONAL MONUMENT, **Fort Frederica**.

WE ANCHOR JUST BELOW
THE RUINS. AN OLD RAM-
SHACKLE DOCK NEARBY
LOOKS QUITE UNSAFE.
INSTEAD, WE SCRAMBLE
UP THE GOOEY MUD
BANK, TIE THE DINGHY
PAINTER TO A TREE NEAR
THE REMAINS OF THE POWDER

MAGAZINE. THE FORT ITSELF WASHED INTO THE RIVER LONG AGO.[*]
THE GROUNDS ARE BEAUTIFULLY KEPT, AND THE LITTLE MUSEUM
HAS MADE THE MOST OF THE FEW REMAINING ARTIFACTS. GENERAL
JAMES OGLETHORPE (OUR MAN FROM SAVANNAH) ESTABLISHED THIS
MILITARY OUTPOST (1736), AND NAMED IT AFTER FREDERICK, THE
ONLY SON OF GEORGE II. AT THAT TIME THE POINT OVERLOOKED
ALMOST THE ENTIRE LENGTH OF THE RIVER. THE FORT HAD FOUR
BASTIONS AND WAS CONSTRUCTED OF TABBY (CEMENT MADE OF
LIME, SAND OR GRAVEL, AND OYSTER SHELLS). THE TOWN OF
FREDERICA WAS BUILT BEHIND THE FORT IN A CRESCENT SHAPE;

---

[*] THE MUDDY BANKS HAVE ERODED SO BADLY THAT BOATERS NOW ARE
REQUESTED NOT TO CLIMB THEM. PLANS, HOWEVER, ARE FOR A VISITOR'S
DOCK.

WELL PROTECTED FROM ATTACK BY THICK FORESTS TO THE NORTH AND EAST AND BOGGY RIVER MARSHES TO THE WEST. PLANNED AS A TYPICAL ENGLISH VILLAGE, FREDERICA BOASTED ONCE OF AS MANY AS A THOUSAND INHABITANTS. IN 1742 FIFTY SPANISH VESSELS ANCHORED IN ST. SIMON'S SOUND AND ATTACKED THE ISLAND. OGLETHORPE AMBUSHED THE SPANISH IN THE MARSHES AND KILLED OR WOUNDED MOST OF THEM (THE BATTLE OF BLOODY MARSH). IT WAS THE FINAL CONFLICT BETWEEN THE SPANISH AND ENGLISH FOR SOVEREIGNTY IN GEORGIA. FIRE DESTROYED THE TOWN OF FREDERICA IN 1758.

ON A PREVIOUS VISIT, *SEA WIND'S* CREW HAD GATHERED FIREWOOD FROM THE MAINTENANCE AREA BRUSH PILE, AT THE SUGGESTION OF A RANGER. WE CARRY OUR CANVAS BAG ASHORE IN HOPES OF A REPEAT. THE TINY TOT'S FIREWOOD BOX IS PERILOUSLY LOW. THE RANGER WE ADDRESS IS OBVIOUSLY UPSET BY THE NOTION, SAYS WE MUSTN'T REMOVE AS MUCH AS A TWIG, EYES OUR CANVAS BAG WITH MISTRUST, AND FOLLOWS US ABOUT THE MUSEUM AND RUINS UNTIL WE RETREAT DOWN THE BANK ONCE MORE — FEELING QUITE LIKE MISCREANTS. EIGHT P.M. OF THIS DARK NIGHT, THE HOWL OF A POWERFUL OUTBOARD BRINGS US ON DECK. BRIGHT LIGHTS SHINE INTO THE MARSH NEARBY — GUNSHOTS, AND THE SCREAM OF AN ANIMAL IN PAIN. COON HUNTERS, LIGHTS STRAPPED TO THEIR HEADS; HIGH POWER RIFLES; THE GUNNER INTO THE GRASSES, DRAGGING POOR WOUNDED BEAST OUT AND INTO THE BOAT — AWAY THEY ROAR.

JACKLIGHTING! STRICTLY ILLEGAL, BUT THE GOOD OLD BOYS WILL GO AT IT, HAMMER AND TONG THE WAY THEY'VE ALWAYS DONE.

"*L*IFT AND SLIP, THAT'S MY MOTTO", SAYS THE SKIPPER. A SUNNY DAY'S IN THE OFFING. *SEA WIND*'S AWAY

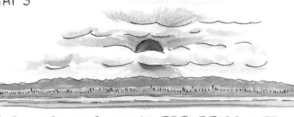

EARLY, TO CATCH THE 8:30 OPENING OF THE FREDERICA LIFT BRIDGE. JUST BEYOND, WE TIE UP AT A MARINA ON LANIER ISLAND TO TAKE FUEL AND TOP UP THE WATER TANKS. WE FIND NO CHAR-COAL (OUR BACK-UP CABIN STOVE FUEL) IN THEIR LITTLE STORE, SO AWAY WE GO UNDER POWER AND SAIL TO CROSS ST. SIMONS SOUND. WHAT BREEZE THERE IS — AT N.W., LEAVES THE SOUNDS UNRUFFLED. THERE'S A QUEER LIGHT ON EVERYTHING (FUMES OF PAPER PULP AND OTHER INDUSTRY IN THE CITY OF BRUNSWICK). WE PASS JEKYLL IS-LAND AND RUN OUT THE LONG DOGLEG INTO ST. ANDREW SOUND. ON

JEKYLL PT. A GROUP OF WET-SUITED NAVY

FROGMEN ARE ENTERING THE WATER. TRAINING MANEUVERS. BRRR! THE CURRENT FAVORS US UNTIL THE SEA BUOY, AFTER WHICH WE MUST STEM IT — A LONG, SLOW PUSH TO CUMBERLAND DIVIDINGS AND THROUGH THE KINGS BAY COMPLEX. SO MUCH ACTIVITY GOES ON HERE (KINGS BAY SUBMARINE BASE) THAT THE NAVIGATIONAL AIDS SEEM TO BE IN A CONSTANT STATE OF FLUX. IT'S A CHALLENGE TO SORT IT ALL OUT. PAST DRUM PT. ISLAND AND BIG MARSH ISLAND, THEN *SEA WIND* ROUNDS UP AND ANCHORS NEAR THE NATIONAL PARK DOCK ON CUMBER-LAND ISLAND. WE'VE PASSED UP SOME OF THESE SEA ISLANDS, BUT MEAN TO GIVE CUMBERLAND A GOOD GO.

IN ST. SIMONS SOUND, OUT OF PANAMA

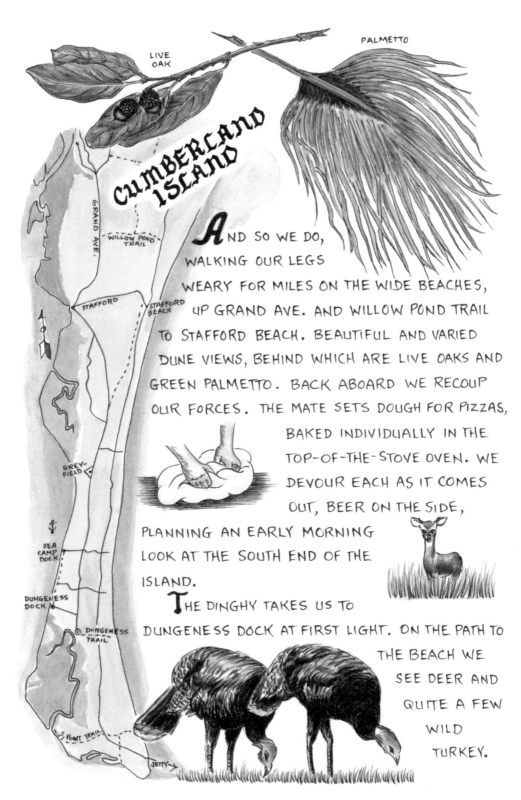

LIVE OAK

PALMETTO

GRAND AVE.

WILLOW POND TRAIL

STAFFORD

STAFFORD BEACH

GREY-FIELD

SEA CAMP DOCK

DUNGENESS DOCK

DUNGENESS TRAIL

S POINT TRAIL

JETTY

CUMBERLAND ISLAND

And so we do, walking our legs weary for miles on the wide beaches, up Grand Ave. and Willow Pond Trail to Stafford Beach. Beautiful and varied dune views, behind which are live oaks and green palmetto. Back aboard we recoup our forces. The mate sets dough for pizzas, baked individually in the top-of-the-stove oven. We devour each as it comes out, beer on the side, planning an early morning look at the south end of the island.

The dinghy takes us to Dungeness Dock at first light. On the path to the beach we see deer and quite a few wild turkey.

WE LOOK OVER THE MUSEUM
AND WANDER ABOUT THE
RUINS OF DUNGENESS, A
FORMER MANSION OF THE
CARNEGIE FAMILY, WHO HAD
ACQUIRED MOST OF THE
ISLAND IN THE LATE 1800'S,
AND USED IT AS AN EX-
CLUSIVE WINTER PLAYGROUND.

MY, IT WAS A HANDSOME PLACE. UNBELIEVABLE CONTRASTS BETWEEN
THESE BARONIAL ESTATES, THE WAY THE
WEALTHY RESIDED
AND THE SUBSISTENCE
LIVING OF NEARBY
FARMERS AND FISHER-
MEN.

IRON WINDOW GRATING DETAIL

OF COURSE, THAT WEALTH
KEPT THIS ISLAND PRISTINE
THROUGH THE
YEARS UNTIL THE
GOVERNMENT
ACQUIRED IT.
AS CUMBERLAND
ISLAND NATIONAL
SEASHORE, ITS BEAUTY
CAN NOW BE ENJOYED
BY ANYONE.

PERGOLA IN
COVERED GARDEN
WALK - DOMES,
BALLS AND ARCHES
ABOUND

Florida

HERE WE COME! THE LAST GIFT FROM GEORGIA IS THE SIGHT OF A MINK ON SHORE NEAR THE SOUTH END OF CUMBERLAND ISLAND. THEN A FAVORING CURRENT HURRIES US ACROSS CUMBERLAND SOUND. FERNANDINA BEACH, WITH ITS PULP PLANT SPEWING ODORS, HOLDS NO LURE FOR *SEA WIND* TODAY. WE CARRY ON UNDER POWER AS THE DAY TURNS GREY, CROSSING NASSAU SOUND AND THREADING SAWPIT CREEK UNTIL WE COME TO THE FT. GEORGE RIVER. THIS LOOKS INTERESTING. THERE'S A NICE POOL OF DEEP WATER OFF THE BACK OF LITTLE TALBOT ISLAND, A PERFECT ANCHOR- AGE IF WE CAN SLIP OVER A TWO- FOOT SPOT ON THE RISING TIDE. AFTER SCOUTING AHEAD IN THE DINGHY, WE ACHIEVE OUR GOAL, ANCHORING PAST MARKER "8". IT'S SPITTING RAIN AND COMING ON TO BLOW. WE SNUG IN BELOW, HAVE A HOT BUTTERED RUM AND CREAM UP SOME TUNA TO HAVE ON TOAST FOR SUPPER.

ORNING COMES FOGGY, QUIET, GREY, AND DRIPPING. ON THE VHF BOATS ARE TALKING ABOUT THE GENERALLY POOR RUNNING CONDITIONS – PLENTY OF LOW-TIDE GROUNDINGS. ONE SAILBOAT, APPARENTLY HAVING AN INFLATED IDEA OF THE COAST GUARD'S ELECTRONIC PROWESS, REPORTS ITSELF AS BEING LOST AND

AGROUND, AND RE-
QUESTS TO BE TOLD WHERE
IT IS SO IT CAN BE RES-
CUED. WE'RE IN
NO HURRY. EX-
PLORE THE BEACH
ON LITTLE TALBOT.

FOGGY LITTLE
TALBOT ISLAND

PROBE HOLES IN THE SAND TO FIND A NICE BUNCH OF QUAHOGS.
WE'LL HAVE A GOOD CHOWDER FOR DINNER,
THICK WITH CLAMS. WE KEEP AN OLD GAL-
VANIZED HAND GRINDER ABOARD WHICH
WILL REDUCE THESE LARGE TOUGH
FELLOWS TO CHEWABLE BITS. THE
FLAVOR WILL BE SUPERB.

THE AFTERNOON IS CLEAR ENOUGH
FOR AN EXCURSION BY DINGHY TO THE
KINGSLEY PLANTATION (ON THE FT. GEORGE ISLAND
SIDE). THE SKIPPER'S MIDDLE NAME IS KINGSLEY, SO
HE HAS A SPECIAL INTEREST. WE BEACH THE DINK AND
WALK UP THROUGH THE GROUNDS. THIS IS A STATE HISTORIC SITE WITH THE
OLDEST EXISTING PLANTATION HOUSE IN FLORIDA. SCOTSMAN ZEPHANIAH
KINGSLEY BOUGHT THE PLANTATION IN 1817. HE WAS A SLAVE TRADER, A
CURIOUS IRONY, SINCE HE WROTE DEFENSES OF THE RIGHTS OF FREEDMEN.
HE THOUGHT SLAVERY A NECESSARY EVIL; TOOK THE BLACK DAUGHTER
(ANNA JAI) OF AN EAST AFRICAN TRIBAL CHIEF TO WIFE; OWNED BOATS THAT
WENT UP AND DOWN THE ST. JOHNS RIVER, TRANSPORTING PEOPLE, AND
CARRYING GOODS TO TRADE AND SELL TO PLANTATION OWNERS. WE LOOK
OVER THE GRACIOUS OLD BUILDINGS. DOWN THE ROAD ARE THE REMAINS
OF THE SLAVE QUARTERS. THEN IT'S BACK ABOARD FOR OUR CHOWDER.

A HOP, SKIP AND JUMP FROM HERE IS THE

ST. JOHNS RIVER

JACKSONVILLE ◉

NOW HERE'S A CHANCE! TO FOLLOW THIS NORTH-
WARD-FLOWING RIVER INTO THE HEART OF
FLORIDA MIGHT GIVE US A TASTE OF THE WAY IT USED
TO BE, A TASTE WHETTED BY A READING OF WILLIAM
BARTRAM'S "TRAVELS".

*B*ARTRAM WAS A NATURALIST AND NATURE ARTIST.
(HIS FATHER, JOHN, WAS THE FIRST NATIVE AMERICAN
BOTANIST, NOTED FOR HIS EXPLORATION OF
VIRGIN FORESTS.) JOHN BARTRAM
AND HIS SON EXPLORED
FLORIDA 1765-66. WILLIAM
RETURNED 1773-77 AND
KEPT A JOURNAL WHICH BE-
CAME "BARTRAM'S TRAVELS".
HE USED THE ST. JOHNS RIVER
AS A MEANS TO PENETRATE
"GREAT FORESTS AND
SWAMPS". HE DESCRIBED
WHAT HE SAW MINUTELY:
THE FLORA AND FAUNA; THE
TEEMING NUMBERS OF FISH
AND SHELLFISH; THOUSANDS
OF SEA FOWL — "MANY DIF-
FERENT KINDS LODGING TO-
GETHER"; VAST ORANGE
GROVES; GIANT LIVE OAKS;
LOFTY CYPRESS TREES;
REMAINS OF ABORIGINAL
SETTLEMENTS

PALATKA •

CRESCENT
LAKE

LAKE
GEORGE

BLUE
SPRINGS

AFTER
BARTRAM'S
BREAM

SANFORD •

- 70 -

WITH HUGE TUMULI AND MOUNDS OF
SHELLS; GREAT NUMBERS OF DEER,
TURKEY, BEAR, WOLVES, WILDCAT,
SQUIRREL, RACCOON, AND OPOSSUM.
SOUTH OF LAKE GEORGE, HE CAME
UPON SUCH NUMBERS OF ALLIGATORS

ALLIGATORS
AFTER
BARTRAM

"YOU MIGHT WALK ASHORE ON THEIR HEADS". THEIR ROARING AND
AGGRESIVE DEMEANOR KEPT HIM AWAKE IN HIS CAMPSITE THROUGH
THE NIGHT.

SEA WIND'S CREW IS WITH CHILD TO DISCOVER A
TRACE OF THESE WONDERS. SHE TURNS WEST. WHERE BARTRAM
FOUND A TRADING POST AND PLANTATIONS, WE FIND
SKYSCRAPERS, INDUSTRIAL WORKS,
AND LOTS OF BIG SHIPPING. WE NOTE
SHIP NAMES: *GYPSUM KING* (LONDON),
OLYMPIC GRACE (MONROVIA), *GLOBE
MARATIMA* (GIBRALTAR), *ARAB HAWK*
(LIBERIA). AND TUGS TOO: *SEA
WOLF, WARRIOR, EXPLORER,
PATRIARCH*
(ALL OUT OF
SAN FRANCISCO).
ALSO *POWER-
FUL, MARY
CLAIR,* AND
GATOR MISS.
OUR FAVORITE

Jacksonville

INDEPENDENT LIFE.

TUG IS *ELSBETH* - WELL-KEPT BLACK HULL, YELLOW STRAKE, AND A VARNISHED HOUSE - TOPPED OFF WITH A CROW'S NEST MADE OUT OF A BARREL.

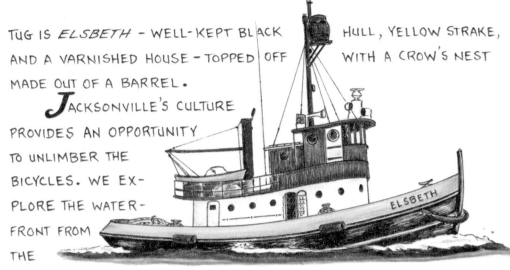

JACKSONVILLE'S CULTURE PROVIDES AN OPPORTUNITY TO UNLIMBER THE BICYCLES. WE EX- PLORE THE WATER- FRONT FROM THE MUNICIPAL MARINA, THEN MOVE TO DOCKS IN THE MORE PROTECTED ORTEGA RIVER AND CONTINUE OUR CITY TOURING OF ART MUSEUMS, LIBRARY, SHOPS, ET AL. THIS IS A GOOD PLACE TO REPLENISH THE SHIP'S STORES. WHEN WE MOVE OFF TO ANCHOR LATE ONE AFTER- NOON, BILLY, LIBERATED FROM THE CABIN WHERE HE'S BEEN KEPT WHILE DOCKSIDE, SPENDS THE NIGHT ON DECK.

A GRAND SAIL UP THE ST. JOHNS (SOUTH!) BRINGS US TO AN ANCHORAGE BELOW RACY PT. WE PICK UP SOME STOVE WOOD ALONG THE BEACH AS REPORTS ARE OF A STRONG NORTHER APPROACHING. THE RIVER IS WIDE IN THESE STRETCHES, THE SHORES PASTORAL. WITH THE TOWN OF **Palatka** AS OUR NEXT DESTINATION, IT'S IN SHEETS TO BEAT UP THE RIVER BENDS, OUR WAKE SWISHING BE- HIND US. WE SLIDE UNDER THE PALATKA BRIDGE AND ANCHOR IN GOOD MUD OFF THE MARINA. A MOST ATTRACTIVE SMALL WATER- FRONT. PALATKA HAS A LARGE PAPER MILL, WHOSE ESSENCE PERVADES

THE AREA. THE LOCALS, NATURALLY, CALL IT THE SMELL OF MONEY. WE WANDER AROUND TOWN; THEN RETIRE TO *SEA WIND* WHERE THE SKIPPER SURROUNDS HIMSELF WITH PRIMUS KEROSENE BURNER PARTS AND REPAIRS OUR AILING COOK STOVE.

*W*HEN WE RISE IT'S COLD, COLD. TEMPERATURE ON DECK IN THE LOW THIRTIES. WE BLESS AND STOKE THE TINY TOT! ASHORE WE BUY CHARTS

FOR UPSTREAM EXPLORATION. FACES NUMB AND THE WIND WASPISH. ICE ON THE DINGHY PAINTER AND ICICLES HANGING FROM THE END OF THE DOCK. A GOOD NIGHT FOR STEW.

*C*OLD OR NO, AWAY WE GO TO FIND ALTERNATING SCENES OF WILD RIVER, NICE HOMES AND PAST WELAKA-FISH CAMPS. THE DAY WARMS. THE MATE SETS BREAD WHILE THE SKIPPER BRINGS US ALONG TO SET THE HOOK

NEAR THE UPPER END OF *Lake George* BETWEEN BLACK PT. AND HOG ISLAND. DOZENS OF BIG SQUIFFY "BLIND MOSQUITOES" COVER THE DECK AND CABIN TOP (THEY DON'T BITE, BUT LOOK LIKE MOSQUITOES). BILLY EAGERLY LAPS THEM UP.

A RAINY MORNING MAKES THE CREW TAKE IT SLOW. READ, EAT. BILLY SITS OUT IN THE RAIN; THEN SETTLES HIS SOPPING SELF ON A PILE OF BEDDING TO TAKE HIS EASE. LEISURE ENOUGH TO MAKE A LEMON-MERINGUE PIE. WE MOVE *SEA WIND* FURTHER INTO THE BAY, EXPECTING A WIND SHIFT OVERNIGHT. WHEN THE RAIN LETS UP, WE ROW THE DINGHY TO LOOK AT A BAIT NET SET UP IN THE SHALLOWS, AND UP A CREEK... LIVE OAK, CYPRESS, CEDAR, PALMETTO, AND THE SPANISH MOSS* HANGING GHOSTLY FROM SO MANY TREES. COLORS MUTED AND GREY. SMELL OF ROTTING THINGS – DARK STUMPS HIDDEN IN THE BLACK WATER. THE EVENING GOES QUIET (THE CALM BEFORE THE STORM) AND ALL WE HEAR ARE BIRD SOUNDS: DUCKS FLAPPING AND TALKING ON THE WATER. A VIBRANT HOOTING (BARRED OWL?) ISOLATED AND WILD ALL RIGHT. THERE ARE MANY SWALLOWS FLITTING ON THE WATER, FEASTING ON OUR SQUIFFY "MOSQUITOES".

*SPANISH MOSS IS NEITHER SPANISH NOR A MOSS. IT'S A NATIVE EPIPHYTE – AIR DWELLING. MORE THAN JUST AESTHETIC, IT IS BROWSED BY CATTLE AND DEER IN THE WINTER. UNTIL THE ADVENT OF SYNTHETICS, IT WAS USED TO STUFF MATTRESSES, SADDLES, CHAIRS – AND WAS WORKED INTO CABLES. TO RENDER IT USEFUL, IT WAS THROWN INTO SHALLOW PONDS EXPOSED TO THE SUN. THE OUTSIDE FURRY SUBSTANCE ROTTED AND DISSOLVED. AFTER BEING DRIED, BEATEN AND SHAKEN, A HARD, BLACK ELASTIC ENTANGLED FILAMENT RESEMBLING HORSEHAIR REMAINED.

-74-

THREE A.M. HOWLING WIND AND RAIN. AT DAWN ONLY THE RAIN CONTINUES, THE WIND LIGHT AND SOUTHERLY, THE TEMPERATURE MILD. THE FORE-CAST IS FOR CLEARING AND BY NINE THINGS LOOK GOOD ENOUGH FOR US TO SAIL AWAY UNDER JIB AND MIZZEN; THE GREY SKIES SPLOTCHY WITH BLUE. OUT IN LAKE GEORGE, THE WIND'S STILL SOUTH. THE SKIPPER SETS THE MAIN TO MAKE GOOD TIME CROSSING THIS TEN-MILE-LONG LAKE. BUT A WIND SHIFT WITH HEAVY WEATHER CATCHES US — LAYS US RIGHT OVER. TIME TO HAND THE MAIN. THE NUMBER TWO JIB IS TOO MUCH AS WELL. SOON WE'RE PITCHING INTO HEAVY SEAS. STRONG GUSTS — UP AROUND FORTY KNOTS WE SUSPECT. A NORTHERLY GALE IS JAMMING US DOWN TOWARD THE SOUTH END OF THE LAKE WHERE WE MUST FIND A VERY NARROW EXIT ACROSS THE VOLUSIA BAR AND THROUGH A WIRE WATER-HYACINTH FENCE. WITH ALL THE SPINDRIFT FLYING, IT'S DIFFICULT TO LOCATE. ANXIETY UNTIL WE SIGHT THE MARKERS. BEYOND, LOTS OF WATER HYACINTHS. THEY FILL THE WATERWAY AS FAR AS THE ANCHOR-AGE WE CHOOSE IN MORRISON CREEK. WIND'S HOWLING AND GREY GURF BLOWING THE PALMS INSIDE OUT! A BITTER COLD NIGHT.

ICE ON DECK COME DAWN. ICICLES HANGING FROM THE HASTILY FURLED MAINS'L.

WATER
HYACINTH

TEMPERATURE IN THE UPPER TWENTIES. WE LIKE A WINTER CRUISE, BUT THIS IS ARCTIC! LOTS OF DAMAGE TO THE CITRUS CROP FROM THIS. THE SUN IS OUT AND THOUGH WE START OFF WITH MUFFLERS AND MITTIES, WE'RE SOON WARM WITHOUT THEM. THEN THERE'S THIS GRAND STRETCH OF RIVER. LONG REACHES WITH NO HABITATION. PAST OLD PLANTATION SITES: ASTOR, BLUFFTON, IDLEWILD, HAPPY HILL, AND ON UP THE RIVER. IN AN OLD LOOP OFF MARKER "75" (JUST PAST BLUE SPRINGS) WE FIND A PERFECT ANCHORAGE. CYPRESS AND GRASSES AND WATER HYACINTHS.* THE LIGHT TODAY IS REMARKABLE. THIS IS WHAT WE CAME FOR. BIRDS — OSPREY, TURKEY VULTURES, KING RAIL, PURPLE GALLINULE, ANHINGA, ROUGH-LEGGED HAWK, LOTS OF GREAT EGRETS, GREAT BLUE HERON, LITTLE BLUE HERON.

GREAT
EGRET

BLUE
SPRINGS

TURKEY VULTURES' WING TIPS TURN UP

* THE UBIQUITOUS WATER HYACINTH, BROUGHT FROM VENEZUELA IN 1884 AND INTRODUCED INTO THE ST. JOHNS RIVER BY A LADY WHO THOUGHT THE PURPLE FLOWER WOULD EMBELLISH HER WATERFRONT, IS NOW BECOME A TROUBLE- SOME WEED. IT CHOKES THE NAVIGABLE CHANNELS. MANATEES FEED ON IT (DEER TOO), BUT STILL IT GROWS. LARGE EXPENDITURES OF LABOR AND MONEY ON MECHANICAL AND CHEMICAL CONTROL RESULT IN ONLY TEM- PORARY RELIEF.

THE GREY WINTER SHORE IS DECORATED BY BALLS OF GREEN MISTLETOE AND TOUCHES OF RED (MAPLE-SEED PODS). AT THIS LATITUDE THE WEATHER MODERATES VERY QUICKLY AFTER A NORTHER, AND BY THE TIME WE ENTER LAKE MONROE, WE'RE DOWN TO SHIRTSLEEVES AGAIN. THE WATER'S THINNER HERE AND WE TIPTOE ACROSS THE LAKE TO *Sanford*, WHERE WE LIE AT THE MUNICIPAL MARINA'S TRANSIENT DOCK FOR A COUPLE OF DAYS. SANFORD IS IN THE MIDST OF FARMING COUNTRY. IT'S AN EASY WALK TO TOWN. OUR IMPRESSION IS OF A QUIET, OLD-FASHIONED PLACE.

           SOUTH OF LAKE MONROE THE ST. JOHNS IS TOO SHALLOW FOR OUR FOUR AND A HALF FOOT DRAFT, SO SANFORD IS OUR TERMINUS. WHEN WE HEAD NORTH (DOWN THE RIVER), THE EDGES OF LAKE MONROE LOOK SOFT WITH LOTS OF MARSH GRASS. SKIPPER SAYS IT REMINDS HIM OF MIDWEST LAKES.

It's A SUNNY, MILD AFTERNOON WHEN WE ANCHOR NEAR BLUE SPRINGS. A PARK ASHORE WITH A BOARDWALK AROUND THE SPRINGS ALLOWS US TO VIEW AN ENTIRE HERD OF MANATEES HARBORING FROM THE CHILLED RIVER IN THE CLEAR WARM SPRING WATER. THE CREATURES HAVE CERTAIN CHARACTERISTICS THAT INDICATE THEY MAY BE DISTANTLY RELATED TO ELEPHANTS. SINCE THEY MOVE SO SLOWLY, THEY'RE AT RISK FROM MOTOR BOAT PROPELLERS.

SEA WIND MAKES ANOTHER STOP IN A STREAM PAST HONTOON PARK. ASHORE WE SEE THE REPLICA OF AN OWL TOTEM CARVED OVER SIX HUNDRED YEARS AGO (THE LARGEST ARTIFACT EVER FOUND IN SOUTH FLORIDA). AN EIGHTY-FOOT WATCH TOWER GIVES A NEW PERSPECTIVE ON THE MARSH, RIVER, AND SWAMP COUNTRY. FURTHER UP THE CREEK (BY DINGHY) WE LOOK AT A CEREMONIAL TIMUCUAN INDIAN MOUND, FIFTEEN TO TWENTY FEET HIGH. WE ANCHOR FOR THE NIGHT IN A CUTOFF NEAR MARKER "30". THE SKIPPER TAKES A SWIM. THE NICE WEATHER HAS BROUGHT OUT A LOT OF SMALL FISHING BOATS.

A GOOD FORECAST SPURS US TO AN EARLY START UNDER POWER. PERFECT REFLECTIONS IN THE RIVER; WE BREAKFAST

UNDER WAY. LAKE GEORGE IS FLAT CALM THIS TIME, PROVIDING THE OPPORTUNITY TO ANCHOR OFF THE SHORE NEAR SILVER GLEN SPRING. WE EXPLORE BY DINGHY. THE CREEK HAS A BEAUTIFUL ENTRANCE AND THE SPRING IS NOT FAR IN, BUT IT'S PROTECTED BY A ROPE AND "PRIVATE" SIGNS. HOWEVER, THE WATER IS CLEAR AND ENTICING, WITH MANY, MANY FISH.

FLORIDA COOTER

LOTS OF TURTLES SUNNING THEMSELVES ON LOGS IN THE GRASSES, AND ONE ALLIGATOR. SKIPPER CAN'T STAND IT AND RETRIEVES HIS FINS AND FACE PLATE FROM *SEA WIND* TO SLIP IN AND TAKE A MORE INTIMATE LOOK. HE HAS A NICE LITTLE DRIFT ALONGSIDE THE DINGHY UNTIL A WATER SNAKE SWIMS BY HIS NOSE, CAUSING A HURRIED LEAP ABOARD. *SEA WIND* UNDER WAY ONCE MORE DOWN RIVER AS FAR AS THE SEVEN SISTERS, TO ANCHOR BETWEEN TROUT ISLAND AND ITS NEIGHBOR TO THE NORTH. IT'S A PRETTY SPOT WHICH TREATS US TO OWL HOOTS OF SEVERAL KINDS.

WE REVISIT *Palatka* AND CYCLE ALL OVER....TO THE CHAMBER OF COMMERCE, LIBRARY, ACROSS THE BRIDGE, AROUND RESIDENTIAL AREAS, AND UP TO RAVINE STATE GARDENS, (A PARK WITH MORE THAN ONE HUNDRED ACRES OF RAVINES WITH NATURE TRAILS, ATTRACTIVE PLANTINGS, STREAMS, PICNIC SITES).

HUGE, HOOP-SHAPED FUNNEL NET TRAPS CATFISH NEAR PALATKA

*E*N ROUTE TO JACKSONVILLE, MILD SOUTHERLY BREEZES HELP US DOWN RIVER (NORTH). WE MAKE AN INTERMEDIATE STOP IN A COVE OFF CLARK CREEK (WEST SIDE OF THE RIVER). THIS SHOULD GIVE US GOOD PROTECTION FROM A PRE- DICTED FRONT, WHICH PASSES IN THE NIGHT RE- SULTING IN STRONG W N W WINDS (HEADWINDS FOR US), SO WE STAY OVER A DAY IN THIS BEAUTIFUL SPOT. SKIPPER CHANGES ENGINE OIL AND TUNES THINGS UP. NEW ROLLERS ARE NEEDED AT THE SPREADER TIPS, AND IN THE AFTERNOON HE DIVES TO SCRUB THE HULL AND CLEAN THE LOG ROTOR. THE MATE IS KNOTTING A BOTTLE (TO KEEP IT FROM CLANKING IN THE LOCKER).

VULTURE TREE

A LAST DAY IN **Jacksonville** ROUNDS OUT OUR ST. JOHNS RIVER FORAY. A RICH EXPERIENCE. WE PAID WITH ICE AND STORM WINDS FOR A DE- LIGHTFULLY DESERTED WINTER RIVER, MORE TO OUR LIKING THAN SUMMER'S HEAVY WATER TRAFFIC, HEAT, HUMIDITY AND REAL MOSQUITOES.

WHEN WE REJOIN THE ICW, WE LOOK SOUTH TO A DIF-
FERENT KIND OF CRUISING: THE WIDE UNINHABITED COASTAL
MARSHES THROUGH WHICH THE WATERWAY WINDS IN THE MID-AT-
LANTIC STATES NOW GIVE WAY TO A WATERWAY, PASSING, AS
OFTEN AS NOT, THROUGH DEVELOPED LAND. FLORIDA IS, AFTER
ALL, A POPULOUS STATE WITH HEAVILY-DEVELOPED COASTS. AS
THE CLIMATE WARMS, SO DOES THE ACTIVITY ALONG THE WATER'S
EDGE INCREASE. BURGEONING URBAN AREAS, MORE MARINAS,
MORE BRIDGES (FOR MORE HIGHWAYS), AND MORE WATERCRAFT
OF ALL KINDS. CONSEQUENTLY, FEWER ANCHORAGES, CRAMPING *SEA
WIND'S* USUAL STYLE OF SEARCHING OUT THE REMOTE PLACES. BUT
CONGESTED AREAS PROVIDE SHARPNESS OF CONTRAST, PLUS EASIER
ACCESS TO MUSEUMS, GALLERIES, LIBRARIES, CONCERTS AND, OF
COURSE, PROVISIONS.

FLORIDA IS THE END OF THE RAINBOW FOR SOME. IT'S A
LOVELY FEELING TO PUT AWAY THE WINTER CLOTHES AND SAIL WITH
A WARM SUN OVERHEAD. THE NORTHERS LOSE THEIR PUNCH. WE
WILL SAVOR THE WIDER WATERS OF MOSQUITO LAGOON, THE
INDIAN RIVER, BISCAYNE BAY; LOOK FORWARD TO RUBBER-
NECKING WATERFRONT DWELLINGS WHETHER PALACES OR
FUNKY SHACKS; THE MAD MELEE OF BOATING BETWEEN FT.
LAUDERDALE AND MIAMI; DOWN THE CRYSTAL WATERS OF THE
KEYS; OFFSHORE TO THAT BEAUTIFUL PUNCTUATION POINT AT
THE END OF THE EAST COAST INTRACOASTAL WATERWAY, THE
DRY TORTUGAS; NORTH ALONG THE SHORES OF THE EVERGLADES
TO FT. MYERS; AND THEN THROUGH THE STILL-WILD, ALMOST
TROPICAL BEAUTY OF THE CALOOSAHATCHEE RIVER, LAKE
OKEECHOBEE AND THE ST. LUCIE CANAL AND RIVER, THUS COM-
PLETING A CIRCUMNAVIGATION OF SOUTH FLORIDA.

On the way to St. Augustine: cream and gold grasses at the water's edge; sand bars; lots of birds.

Two bald eagles — one immature.

A wood stork poking his long bill into the mud looking for goodies.

Sea Wind pays the penalty of sitting aground an hour and a half in Palm Valley Cut for giving a tug with barge too wide a berth.

Tolomato River. Clouds boil up from the east. *Sea Wind* seeks shelter in a loop out of the waterway at Pine Island. The VHF gives a tornado watch. A hard squall line moves in bringing winds of 40 knots. Black clouds roll over, then leave us in a grey and dripping calm.

PINE ISL.

TOLOMATO RIVER

St. Augustine

OLD SPANISH CITY FOUNDED CIRCA 1565. ACQUIRED BY THE U.S. IN 1821. RED-TILED ROOFS AND TURRETS BECKON. THOUGH EN-CRUSTED WITH TOURISM, ITS AUTHENTICITY SAVES IT. NUMEROUS SHRINES, MUSEUMS, CHURCHES, AND FINE RESTAURANTS ARE WITHIN WALKING DISTANCE OF THE DOWNTOWN MARINA. OIL MAG-NATE HENRY FLAGLER BUILT (IN THE LATE 1800'S) LUXURY HOTELS (ONE NOW A MUSEUM; ONE A COLLEGE), AND A MAGNIFICENT PRESBYTERIAN CHURCH, A MEMORIAL TO HIS DAUGHTER.

CROISSANTS FROM A NEARBY PATISSERIE - RUN BY A GENUINE FRENCHMAN - DUNKED IN OUR COFFEE, HELP US SLIP INTO THE DAY.

BRIDGE OF LIONS

ON HOLIDAYS, FLAGS FLY FROM ALL THE LIGHT POLES

LIONS THAT LOOK LIKE BERT LEHR GUARD THE BRIDGE

ON THE DOCKS RUDDY TURN-STONES SO TAME WE FEED THEM CRUMBS AND BOSSY

8-10"

BOAT-TAILED GRACKLE

16-17"

IN THE MID 1600'S THE SPANISH BUILT THE FORTRESS

CASTILLO DE SAN MARCOS

-83-

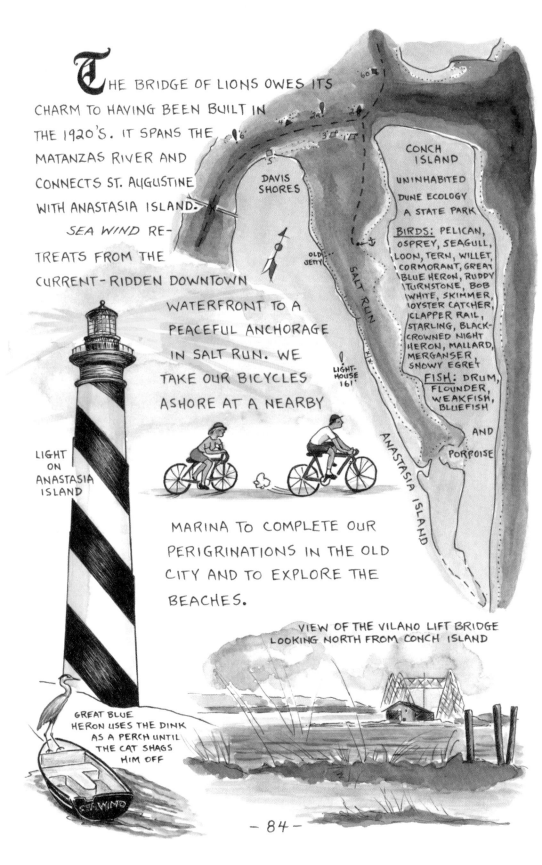

$\mathcal{T}$HE BRIDGE OF LIONS OWES ITS CHARM TO HAVING BEEN BUILT IN THE 1920'S. IT SPANS THE MATANZAS RIVER AND CONNECTS ST. AUGUSTINE WITH ANASTASIA ISLAND.

SEA WIND RE-TREATS FROM THE CURRENT-RIDDEN DOWNTOWN WATERFRONT TO A PEACEFUL ANCHORAGE IN SALT RUN. WE TAKE OUR BICYCLES ASHORE AT A NEARBY MARINA TO COMPLETE OUR PERIGRINATIONS IN THE OLD CITY AND TO EXPLORE THE BEACHES.

DAVIS SHORES

CONCH ISLAND

UNINHABITED DUNE ECOLOGY A STATE PARK

<u>BIRDS</u>: PELICAN, OSPREY, SEAGULL, LOON, TERN, WILLET, CORMORANT, GREAT BLUE HERON, RUDDY TURNSTONE, BOB WHITE, SKIMMER, OYSTER CATCHER, CLAPPER RAIL, STARLING, BLACK-CROWNED NIGHT HERON, MALLARD, MERGANSER SNOWY EGRET

<u>FISH</u>: DRUM, FLOUNDER, WEAKFISH, BLUEFISH AND PORPOISE

OLD JETTY

SALT RUN

LIGHTHOUSE 161'

ANASTASIA ISLAND

LIGHT ON ANASTASIA ISLAND

VIEW OF THE VILANO LIFT BRIDGE LOOKING NORTH FROM CONCH ISLAND

GREAT BLUE HERON USES THE DINK AS A PERCH UNTIL THE CAT SHAGS HIM OFF

SEA WIND

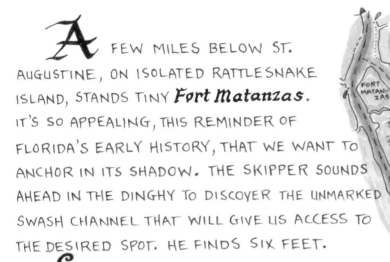

$\mathcal{A}$ FEW MILES BELOW ST. AUGUSTINE, ON ISOLATED RATTLESNAKE ISLAND, STANDS TINY *Fort Matanzas.* IT'S SO APPEALING, THIS REMINDER OF FLORIDA'S EARLY HISTORY, THAT WE WANT TO ANCHOR IN ITS SHADOW. THE SKIPPER SOUNDS AHEAD IN THE DINGHY TO DISCOVER THE UNMARKED SWASH CHANNEL THAT WILL GIVE US ACCESS TO THE DESIRED SPOT. HE FINDS SIX FEET.

$\mathcal{E}$VEN THOUGH A PARK SERVICE LAUNCH OCCASION-ALLY BRINGS PEOPLE FROM ANASTASIA ISLAND TO SEE THIS NATIONAL MONU-MENT, IT'S A QUIET SPOT. THE RANGER ASSURES US WE CAN TAKE TWO BUSHELS (PER BOAT) OF THE OYSTERS WE SEE ALONG THE SHORE. WE GATHER ENOUGH FOR A STEW — PLUS A FEW FOR BILLY.

BUILT BY THE SPANISH IN THE MID 1700'S

$\mathcal{F}$ROM THE PARAPET LOOKING DOWN ON OUR LITTLE BOAT AND OVER THE MARSHES, IT'S EASY TO CONJURE UP TURBULENT COLONIAL STRUGGLES FOR POWER AND WEALTH. AT NIGHT, HOW-EVER, THE SURPRISING GLARE OF LIGHTS FROM THE CONDOS NORTH OF MATANZAS INLET REDUCE THE LITTLE FORTIFICATION TO A CIPHER.

HOODED MERGANSER

PORPOISE SHOW AT MARINELAND

*S*EA WIND IS OFF TO *Daytona Beach* ON A PEACH OF A MORNING WITH NICE WORKING NORTHERLY AIRS. WE PASS A CANOE WITH A REAR-VIEW MIRROR (FOR ROWING ON A BUSY WATERWAY); A COUPLE OF CHARACTER SAILBOATS WITH BIZARRE RIGS: A FREEDOM 40 CAT KETCH WITH UNSTAYED MASTS AND WISHBONE BOOMS, AND A KETCH SPORTING A SPRIT-BOOM MAIN AND A FULLY BATTENED LUG MIZZEN.

*W*E ARRANGE WITH A BOATYARD NEAR DAYTONA BEACH TO HAUL *SEA WIND* SO WE CAN CLEAN AND PAINT HER BOTTOM. SHE'LL SLIP ALONG SMOOTHLY FOR ANOTHER YEAR. THE OCEAN, WITH ITS MILES OF MARVELOUS WIDE, FLAT BEACHES, IS JUST A FEW BLOCKS AWAY. ONE EVENING WE TAKE OFF OUR PAINT-SPATTERED OVERALLS, DRESS UP, AND TAKE IN THE DAYTONA BEACH SYMPHONY.... BERLIOZ, MOZART AND TCHAIKOVSKY, CONDUCTED WITH GREAT SPIRIT.

A SATURDAY MORNING VISIT TO THE FARMERS' MARKET PROVIDES US WITH FRESH PRODUCE FOR OUR NEXT LEG SOUTH.

A BIT OF R AND R IS IN ORDER AFTER OUR BOAT-YARD LABORS. BELOW NEW SMYRNA BEACH THE CHART SHOWS A SMALL DEEP CHANNEL TO THE EAST OF MARKER "47". CAREFULLY WE WORK OUT OF THE INTRACOASTAL, A MID-CHANNEL ISLAND ON ONE SIDE, A SAND BAR ON THE OTHER, AND COME TO REST WITH OUR ANCHOR IN EIGHT FEET OF WATER. WE LIE TO A STRONG REVERSING TIDAL CURRENT. THIS SMALL CORNER IS REWARDING IN MANY WAYS. IT GIVES US A MATRIX OF CREEKS TO EXPLORE BY DINGHY AND SIGHTS AND SOUNDS THAT PLEASE US. COCKTAIL TIME FINDS US SURROUNDED BY PORPOISE - LEAPING, TWIRLING, ROLLING, SLAPPING THEIR TAILS, AND BLOWING. CORMORANTS BUNCHED ON A SAND BAR LIKE A GROUP OF LITTLE OLD MEN — HUNCHED, AS IF COLD. THE SAME SAND BAR EARLIER YIELDED QUAHOGS, NOW HUNG OVER THE STERN IN A NET BAG TO PURGE THEIR INSIDES OF SAND.

COMMERCIAL DOCKS AND WORKING BOATS NORTH OF NEW SMYRNA BEACH

SEAFOOD

MY BOYS

MISS EMMA

PROBING FOR CLAMS

Mosquito Lagoon is a wide and shallow sheet of water with a dredged channel. Of waters like this, Henry Plummer said "if you lay flat on your stomach and wait for a spring tide, you might be able to drown....".

In long, straight stretches we're often grateful for our automatic pilot, whose arm, when attached to the tiller, steers the boat, freeing the watch person to leave the helm for short periods, whether to get a cup of tea, study the chart or the constantly changing water scene.

IMMATURE BONAPARTE'S GULL

Mosquito Lagoon, Haulover Canal, and the upper reaches of the *Indian River* are alive with birds; also alive with small fishing boats. In the canal, fishermen try their luck from the banks. Large white pelicans appear. Ponderous birds, handsomely marked, they feed by scooping fish up while swimming. Quite different from their smaller brown relatives' spectacular and smashing plunge into the water from the sky.

SOUTH OF THE ADDISON PT. BRIDGE, THERE'S PLENTY OF WATER FOR *SEA WIND* TO ANCHOR. BILLY RIDES THE DINGHY BOW TO A CAT-SIZED SPOIL ISLAND NEARBY. AFTER HIS LOCK-UP IN THE BOATYARD, HE ACTS A BIT GIDDY, SNIFFING, RUNNING, CLIMBING TREES, AND GENERALLY SPORTING ABOUT.

ADDISON PT.

TWO OR THREE NIGHTS AT ANCHOR IN THE INDIAN RIVER, WE'RE PUZZLED BY MYSTERIOUS TAPPING, DRUMMING, AND THUMPING. WE FINALLY REALIZE THE CAUSE IS A NOISY FISH CALLED A DRUM. THE MESSAGE IS ONLY FULLY UNDERSTOOD BY OTHER DRUMS; ONE THEORY HOLDS IT HAS TO DO WITH COURTSHIP.

GUARDING A POPULAR ANCHORAGE IN THE BANANA RIVER, EAU GALLIE'S STUCCO DRAGON, CREATED AS A LARK BY A RESIDENT, IS NOW A CHARTED LAND-MARK.

PULLING A CLAM RAKE ON A CHILLY MORNING

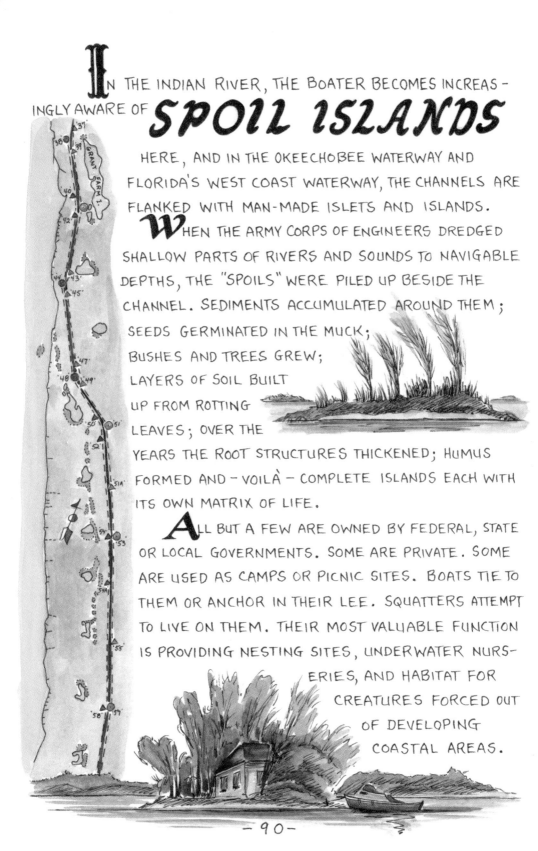

IN THE INDIAN RIVER, THE BOATER BECOMES INCREAS-INGLY AWARE OF **SPOIL ISLANDS** HERE, AND IN THE OKEECHOBEE WATERWAY AND FLORIDA'S WEST COAST WATERWAY, THE CHANNELS ARE FLANKED WITH MAN-MADE ISLETS AND ISLANDS. **W**HEN THE ARMY CORPS OF ENGINEERS DREDGED SHALLOW PARTS OF RIVERS AND SOUNDS TO NAVIGABLE DEPTHS, THE "SPOILS" WERE PILED UP BESIDE THE CHANNEL. SEDIMENTS ACCUMULATED AROUND THEM; SEEDS GERMINATED IN THE MUCK; BUSHES AND TREES GREW; LAYERS OF SOIL BUILT UP FROM ROTTING LEAVES; OVER THE YEARS THE ROOT STRUCTURES THICKENED; HUMUS FORMED AND – VOILÀ – COMPLETE ISLANDS EACH WITH ITS OWN MATRIX OF LIFE.

ALL BUT A FEW ARE OWNED BY FEDERAL, STATE OR LOCAL GOVERNMENTS. SOME ARE PRIVATE. SOME ARE USED AS CAMPS OR PICNIC SITES. BOATS TIE TO THEM OR ANCHOR IN THEIR LEE. SQUATTERS ATTEMPT TO LIVE ON THEM. THEIR MOST VALUABLE FUNCTION IS PROVIDING NESTING SITES, UNDERWATER NURS-ERIES, AND HABITAT FOR CREATURES FORCED OUT OF DEVELOPING COASTAL AREAS.

MANY ARE TINY; SOME CONTAIN SEVERAL ACRES. LAND-BUILDING RED MANGROVES ARCH THEIR ROOTS INTO THE WATER. SALT TOLERANT, THEIR INTER- LACED ROOTS AND BRANCHES SHELTER IN- SECTS, CRABS, FISH, AND WADING BIRDS.

DISHEVELED- LOOKING CASUARINAS GROW THICKLY ON MOST OF FLORIDA'S SPOIL ISLANDS. THIS PERNICIOUS TREE, BROUGHT FROM AUSTRALIA TO FORM WIND AND SALT BREAKS FOR THE EXTENSIVE PINEAPPLE PLANTATIONS WORKED ON THE SHORES OF THE INDIAN RIVER EARLY IN THE CENTURY, HAS BE- COME A PEST. AN AGGRESIVE COLONIZER, IT COVERS THE GROUND WITH SMOTHERING NEEDLES SO NO UNDERSTORY PLANTS CAN SURVIVE. ENVIRONMENTALISTS (SCIENTISTS, VOLUNTEERS, STUDENTS) ARE MAKING AN EF- FORT TO REMOVE CASUARINAS AND OTHER EXOTIC PLANTS FROM SOME SPOIL ISLANDS IN ORDER TO RE-ESTABLISH NATIVE FLORA AND FAUNA.

ong stretches of the Indian River are wide enough to allow a good fetch of wind, giving a sailboat the opportunity to reel off free miles (always supposing a *FAIR* wind!). For interest, the maze of lovely humply-dumply isles passed when threading Indian River Narrows is adorned with pines and palms, marsh and mangrove, and lots of new birds, lovely big Florida ones.

South of Vero Beach, the river is too wide to rubberneck the shores. But evidence of growth is everywhere on the horizon. More cultivated scenery and lots of giant cranes rearing in the distance, mostly on the ocean beaches, building up the blocks that make condos.

There are many marinas for refueling, watering, and provisioning the boat. Many opportunities for visiting other cruisers — some with whom we've been playing leap-frog along the way — comparing notes and yarns about our waterway adventures.

SEA WIND HAS A MEMORABLE SAIL,
REACHING ON A SMART BREEZE PAST FT. PIERCE
TO THE ST. LUCIE INLET. ABOVE AND BELOW
THE INLET, SPEED BOATS ROAR BACK AND
FORTH, THEIR OPERATORS TESTING A FAMOUS MAKE
OF OUTBOARD MOTOR, EARMUFFS ON TO PROTECT THEM
FROM THE CONSTANT NOISE BARRAGE. WHO PROTECTS US!

We SLIP INTO **Manatee Pocket**. THIS HUR-
RICANE HOLE IS AN APPEALING BUT FRAGILE PLACE.
THE SURROUNDING LAND AND TREES FORM GOOD SHEL-
TER. HERE, AS IN ANCHORAGES IN THE ST. LUCIE RIVER
OFF STUART, THE TIME YOU MAY ANCHOR IS LIMITED, THE
RESULT OF A MISBEHAVING FEW CONDEMNING THE
MANY, PLUS THE PRESS OF INCREASING
NUMBERS OF BOATS AND PEOPLE IN-
VADING LIMITED SPACES. MANATEE
POCKET IS A WORKING PORT. DOCKS
FOR COMMERCIAL (MACKEREL, TROUT,
BLUES) FISHING BOATS LINE THE WEST
SIDE OF PORT SALERNO (THE USUAL SMELLS
PERVADE). NICE LOOKING HOMES SPORT
LAWNS STRETCHING TO DOCKS ON THE WATER..

DERELICT IN THE SHALLOWS
BECOMES A PELICANS' ROOST

...RESTAURANTS, MARINAS, AND A BOATYARD
SHOW UP AS YOU TREND TOWARDS THE LITTLE TOWN
OF PORT SALERNO AT THE END OF THE POCKET.

THE TOWN OF **Stuart** IS SIX MILES UP
THE ST. LUCIE RIVER
FROM THE I C W.
FOLLOW THE SOUTH
FORK OF THE

OSPREY
TAKES HIS
BREAKFAST
TO A
NEIGHBOR'S
MASTHEAD

SHANTY FISH BOAT ON THE ST. LUCIE RIVER

ST. LUCIE RIVER AND IT WILL LEAD YOU INTO THE OKEECHOBEE
WATERWAY, THE SHORTCUT TO THE GULF COAST. (*SEA WIND* WILL
FOLLOW THIS PIÈCE DE RÉSISTANCE OF FLORIDA WATERWAYS ON
HER RETURN JOURNEY.)

B ELOW ST. LUCIE
INLET (TO THE ATLANTIC
OCEAN) THE INTRACOASTAL
NARROWS. *Peck Lake*
IS A PLACE WHERE
YACHTS CONGREGATE:

PECK
LAKE
PARK-
OCEAN
SIDE

WEEKENDERS FROM THE STUART AREA, OR CRUISING BOATS

PAUSING FOR A
WHILE. A SHORT

WALK ACROSS JUPITER
ISLAND LEADS TO THE OCEAN
BEACH. TORPEDO-SHAPED MUL-
LET POP OUT OF THE WATER AND
SPLASH BACK
IN. MANATEE
MOTHERS
AND CALVES
MAY TAKE
A NAP
IN THE
SHADOW OF
YOUR HULL.

JUPITER ISLAND

PECK LAKE

PECK
LAKE
REFLECTIONS

A LONG WAIT FOR BRIDGE
MAINTENANCE

*H*OBE SOUND'S EXCLUSIVE HOMES AND THEIR BEAUTIFUL
LANDSCAPING ON THE OCEAN SIDE CONTRAST WITH THE WILDLIFE
REFUGE TO THE WEST. BRIDGES AND WATER TRAFFIC PROLIF-
ERATE EN ROUTE TO LAKE WORTH. JUPITER INLET IN
BETWEEN WITH ITS 146 FT. RED BRICK LIGHTHOUSE,
LOOMING ABOVE AS YOU PASS AND THEN, LAKE WORTH
ITSELF WHERE WE TURN NORTH INTO *Old Port Cove*,

OLD PORT ⚓
COVE
LAKE WORTH
INTRACOASTAL

A FAVORITE GATHERING PLACE
FOR BOATS GOING TO AND
COMING FROM THE BAHAMAS.
IN *West Palm Beach*
WE TREAT OURSELVES TO A
NIGHT AT A MARINA; THEN BICYCLE
ACROSS THE FLAGLER MEMORIAL
BRIDGE TO PALM BEACH,
WHERE WE RIDE AROUND
THE NEIGHBORHOODS
OF THE RICH AND
FAMOUS, AND TAKE
SUNDAY BREAKFAST AT
A SIDEWALK RESTAURANT
.... SUNNY, WARM
AND QUITE
TROPICAL.

POWER PLANT - PORT OF WEST PALM BEACH

WITH A BRIDGE SCHEDULE IN ONE HAND AND THE AIR HORN IN THE OTHER, WE NEGOTIATE THE REMAINING MILES TO *Ft. Lauderdale*, TAKING IN ALL THE WATERFRONT ARCHITECTURE. MULTITUDES OF PLASTIC PINK FLAMINGOS AND JET SKIS. WAKES FROM INNUMERABLE SPEED BOATS REVERBERATE BETWEEN CEMENT BULKHEADS. IT'S A RELIEF TO PULL OUT OF THE FRAY IN ONE OF FORT LAUDERDALE'S CANALS AND TIE SNUGLY TO A FRIEND'S DOCK. THE MORNING LIGHT ON THESE CANALS IS TRULY SPECIAL, WITH PALMS, MANGO AND AVACADO TREES, GARDENIAS, AND ALL THE OTHER TROPICAL FLORA THAT GOES WITH THIS KINDLY CLIMATE. HERE WE CATCH UP ON BOAT CHORES, STOCK THE BOAT, AND EXPLORE THE CANALS OF THIS AMERICAN VENICE, OGLING FROM THE DINGHY THE MANY YACHTS TUCKED AWAY IN THE INTRICATE SYSTEM.

HOT SHOT

FORT LAUDERDALE

PORT EVERGLADES

TRAVELLER'S PALM

OUR THOUGHTS NOW TURN TO THE FLORIDA KEYS. SHRINKING FROM ANOTHER DAY WITH TRAFFIC AND TRAUMA ON THE INTRA-COASTAL TO *miami*, WE OPT FOR AN OCEAN SAIL. WE PICK OUR WEATHER (FOR A FAVORABLE WIND) AND LISTEN TO NOAA WEATHER RADIO FOR INFO ON THE EDGE OF THE NORTHWARD FLOWING GULF STREAM, WHICH CAN BE ANYWHERE FROM A MILE TO TEN MILES OFFSHORE (MAXIMUM VELOCITY CAN EXCEED FOUR KNOTS). WE MIGHT EVEN BE LUCKY ENOUGH TO PICK UP A COUNTERCURRENT.

SO PLEASANT IS THE PORTENT OF A DAY ON THE BRINY, WE HAUL ON THE HALYARDS WITH A RIGHT GOOD WILL. *SEA WIND* LEAVES FT. LAUDERDALE AND TURNS HER HEAD SOUTH ALONG THE BEACHES. THE OPEN WATERS, A MODERATE SEA SWELL, AND THE GOOD LITTLE BOAT BOILING ALONG MAKE THE MILES PASS QUICKLY. ALL TOO SOON WE'RE ENTERING GOVERNMENT CUT WITH ALL ITS BIG SHIPPING.

NOTHING FOR IT BUT TO SEE SOME OF THE MIAMI SIGHTS BEFORE ADVENTURING DOWN THE KEYS, SO WE ANCHOR OFF VIRGINIA KEY NEAR THE SEAQUARIUM. THERE'S A DOCK DESIGNATED FOR DINGHIES, MAKING IT EASY TO GET ASHORE AND SEE THE SHOW — SEA LIONS, DOLPHINS, AND KILLER WHALES. GEARED FOR KIDS, BUT WELL DONE.

VIRGINIA KEY

PLANET OCEAN

SEAQUARIUM

TO MIAMI

TO KEY BISCAYNE

ACROSS THE STREET IS PLANET OCEAN (THEY PUBLISH THE FASCINATING SMALL MAGAZINE CALLED *SEA SECRETS*). THIS IS A USEFUL STOP FOR THE MATE, WHO IS SEARCHING OUT INFORMATION FOR A BOOK ON THE QUEEN CONCH.* AS IS A VISIT TO THE NEARBY UNIVERSITY OF MIAMI SCHOOL OF MARINE SCIENCES, WHOSE WORK ON CONCH MARICULTURE IS PIVOTAL TO THE SUR- VIVAL OF THIS IMPOR- TANT SHELLFISH, ONCE SO PLENTIFUL IN THE FLORIDA KEYS.

A DAY AT MIAMARINA IN THE HEART OF THE CITY, AND A FEW DAYS AT DINNER KEY MARINA ARE SPENT PLAYING TOURIST. WE VISIT VIZCAYA AND BRIEFLY ENJOY THIS COPY OF AN ITALIAN REN- AISSANCE VILLA BUILT BY JAMES DEERING 1914-16. PERIOD ROOMS HAVE EUROPEAN DECORATIVE ARTS FROM THE 14TH TO THE 17TH CEN- TURIES. THE FORMAL GARDENS ARE BEAUTIFUL.

IT'S A SHOCK TO RETURN TO THE STREETS OF MAD, MODERN MIAMI WITH ITS TRASH AND RUSH. WE TAKE IN

*SUBSEQUENTLY PUB- LISHED AS *THE CONCH BOOK*, PEN & INK PRESS, P.O. BOX 235, WICOMICO CHURCH, VA. 22579

VIZCAYA

BABY CONCH

Fairchild Gardens

WITH ITS MULTITUDE OF NATIVE AND IM-
PORTED TROPICAL TREES
AND PLANTS. THE FAITH-
FUL BIKES THEN CARRY US
THROUGH COCONUT GROVE'S SECLUDED
LANES WITH ESTATES AND LUSH
PLANTINGS CHARACTERISTIC OF SOUTH FLORIDA — BANYAN, MAHOGANY,
FLAMBOYANT, MAGNOLIA, HIBISCUS, BOUGAINVILLEA, OLEANDER, AND
POINSETTIA. A FRIEND ENLIGHTENS US
ABOUT THE OCCASIONAL PILES OF FRUIT
AT RESIDENTIAL CURBSIDES (MANGOES
IN THIS CASE): THEY ARE SURPLUS GEN-
EROUSLY OFFERED UP TO PASSERS-BY.
LOVELY BOUNTY!
BICYCLE PATHS ON
SHADED STREETS LEAD
US TO PARROT JUNGLE AND
A BREAKFAST IN THEIR CAFETERIA,
WINDOWS FRAMING THE GAUDY INHABITANTS.
To WHET OUR CRUISING APPETITES,
WE MOVE SOUTH TO **Key Biscayne** AND
ANCHOR IN NO NAME HARBOR, SURROUNDED BY
CAPE FLORIDA STATE RECREATION AREA. IT'S SNUG
HERE, ESPECIALLY SO WITH BLACK SQUALLS PASSING
OUT IN THE OCEAN. WE TAKE OUR EASE IN THE COCKPIT
ACCOMPANIED BY A FLAMING SUNSET AND A SOLDIER
BREEZE THAT MAKES THE TALL CASUARINAS SIGH.

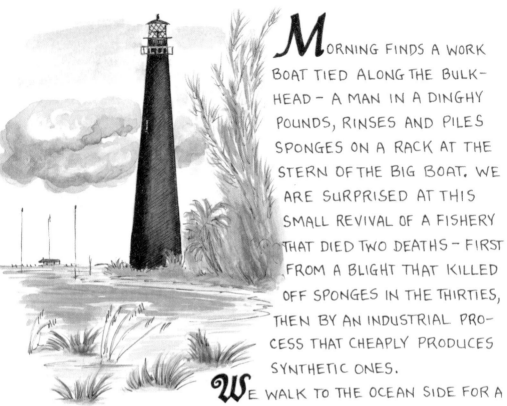

MORNING FINDS A WORK BOAT TIED ALONG THE BULK- HEAD – A MAN IN A DINGHY POUNDS, RINSES AND PILES SPONGES ON A RACK AT THE STERN OF THE BIG BOAT. WE ARE SURPRISED AT THIS SMALL REVIVAL OF A FISHERY THAT DIED TWO DEATHS – FIRST FROM A BLIGHT THAT KILLED OFF SPONGES IN THE THIRTIES, THEN BY AN INDUSTRIAL PRO- CESS THAT CHEAPLY PRODUCES SYNTHETIC ONES.

WE WALK TO THE OCEAN SIDE FOR A BEACHCOMB AND A LOOK AT THE STRIKING CAPE FLORIDA LIGHTHOUSE.

THE FLORIDA KEYS SWEEP 200 MILES FROM HERE TOWARDS THE SOUTHWEST IN A GENTLE CURVE TO THE ISOLATED DRY TORTUGAS. THE SHALLOW WATERS OF FLORIDA BAY ARE TO THE WEST; THE STRAITS OF FLORIDA AND THE DEEP BLUE GULF STREAM TO THE EAST.

THE GULFSTREAM AND PREVAILING SOUTHEAST TRADE WINDS GIVE THE KEYS A NEAR-TROPICAL OCEANIC CLIMATE AND HAVE CAR- RIED PLANT SEEDS FROM THE WEST INDIES TO ENRICH THE AREA. THE ALMOST CONTINUOUS FRINGING REEF IN COMBINATION WITH THE SHALLOW WATERS AND THE CONSTANT CLEANSING BY THE GULF STREAM FOSTERS A SPECTACULAR TRANSLUCENCE – A WINDOW ON NATURE'S SEAQUARIUM.

DRY
TORTUGAS

MARQUESAS

KEY
WEST

THE INTENSE LIGHT OF THIS AREA OF SKY AND WATER GIVES BOATERS THE OPPORTUNITY TO SEE AN ABUNDANCE OF UNDERWATER LIFE. MANY KINDS OF REEF FISH AND MARINE INVERTEBRATES. THE SHALLOWS INSIDE THE REEF ARE A SPAWNING GROUND FOR SMALL FISHES, AND A FEEDING PLACE FOR SHORE AND WATER BIRDS... HERONS, TERNS, OSPREY, GULLS, PELICANS, SPOONBILLS. THIS IS A VERY DIFFERENT EXPERIENCE FROM THE INTRACOASTAL WATERWAY THUS FAR - MORE REMINISCENT OF CRUISING BAHAMIAN WATERS.

BISCAYNE BAY

FLORIDA

FLAMINGO

FLORIDA BAY

HAWK CHANNEL

GULF STREAM

STRAITS OF FLORIDA

OFF KEY BISCAYNE IS AN INTERESTING COLLECTION OF HOUSES BUILT IN THE SHALLOWS ON PILINGS... "STILTSVILLE". THEY ARE AT RISK IN THIS EXPOSED SETTING, AS PROVEN BY PERIODIC HURRICANES. OUR WAY LIES PAST THEM DOWN BISCAYNE BAY, THROUGH FEATHERBED BANK, TO ANCHOR AT *Sands Key*. HERE STARTS THE ROUTINE WE'LL FOLLOW IN THE KEYS: SLIP INTO THE CLEAR WATER WITH MASK, SNORKEL, AND FINS TO SET THE ANCHOR AND EXAMINE THE PRIVATE SEABED AQUARIUM BELOW *SEA WIND'S* HULL. NEARBY ISLETS, BEACHES, AND MANGROVE-LINED CHANNELS INVITE EXPLORATION BY DINGHY. THE BAHAMIAN LOOK BUCKET, IDLE IN A COCKPIT LOCKER FOR MONTHS, COMES INTO FREQUENT USE. THE SUN POURS DOWN, AND WE PROTECT OURSELVES WITH HATS, SUNGLASSES, AND SUN SCREEN.

CARD SOUND, BARNES SOUND, THEN THROUGH JEWFISH CREEK TO ANCHOR IN *Blackwater Sound* SOUTH OF STILLWRIGHT PT. DURING OUR ANCHOR-SETTING AND COOL-OFF SWIM, DISCOVER SCALLOPS UNDER *SEA WIND* AND HARVEST A BUCKETFUL.

WE TOUCH AT PENNEKAMP CORAL REEF
STATE PARK; SPEND A NIGHT IN
TARPON BASIN, BUTTONWOOD SOUND,
TAVERNIER, ISLAMORADA.

Lignumvitae Key IS A PLUM IN
THE FLORIDA KEYS. A PROTECTED STATE
BOTANICAL SITE, IT'S UNIQUE. SOMEHOW DE-
VELOPMENT PASSED THIS 280-ACRE KEY BY
AND THE TREE AND PLANT GROWTH IS OLD... THE ONLY
PLACE IN THIS STRING OF ISLANDS LEFT TO SHOW HOW WILD THE
KEYS WERE WHEN THE SPANIARDS CAME. THE ONLY
ACCESS IS BY WATER. *SEA WIND* FINDS SETTLED
WEATHER, MAKING IT POSSIBLE TO ANCHOR OFF THE
SMALL DOCK AND TAKE A COMPREHENSIVE TOUR.
TREE ROOTS SPREAD WIDE IN THE SPARSE TOPSOIL
OVER THE
LIMESTONE
BASE. THE
RESULT IS
STUNTED
LIKE A
MINIA-
TURE.

TREES: GUMBO LIMBO (A LIGHT
WOOD, LIKE BALSA WITH PEELING RED BARK), LIGNUMVITAE ("WOOD OF
LIFE"-HEAVY AND SINKS-THIS IS ITS NORTHERN LIMIT. VALUABLE BE-
CAUSE OF ITS DENSITY), POISONWOOD
(BLACK-SPOTTED TRUNK - SAP CAUSES SKIN
IRRITATION. WHITE-CROWNED PIGEONS SIT IN
THIS TREE AND EAT ITS BERRIES). JAMAICA

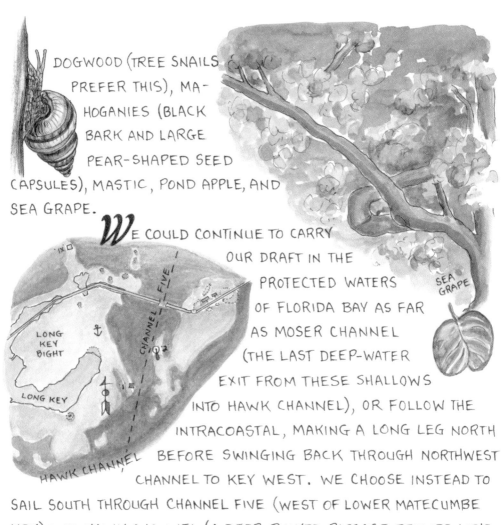

DOGWOOD (TREE SNAILS PREFER THIS), MA-HOGANIES (BLACK BARK AND LARGE PEAR-SHAPED SEED CAPSULES), MASTIC, POND APPLE, AND SEA GRAPE.

SEA GRAPE

LONG KEY BIGHT

LONG KEY

CHANNEL FIVE

HAWK CHANNEL

IX

*W*E COULD CONTINUE TO CARRY OUR DRAFT IN THE PROTECTED WATERS OF FLORIDA BAY AS FAR AS MOSER CHANNEL (THE LAST DEEP-WATER EXIT FROM THESE SHALLOWS INTO HAWK CHANNEL), OR FOLLOW THE INTRACOASTAL, MAKING A LONG LEG NORTH BEFORE SWINGING BACK THROUGH NORTHWEST CHANNEL TO KEY WEST. WE CHOOSE INSTEAD TO SAIL SOUTH THROUGH CHANNEL FIVE (WEST OF LOWER MATECUMBE KEY) INTO HAWK CHANNEL (A DEEP, BUOYED PASSAGE BETWEEN THE OFFSHORE REEFS AND THE KEYS). AND NOW THE SKIPPER MUST BE ESPECIALLY ALERT. THESE ARE TREACHEROUS WATERS WHERE REEFS AND SHALLOWS ABOUND. WELL MARKED TODAY, IT'S EASY TO SEE HOW VESSELS RIDING THE GULF STREAM COULD COME A CROPPER. STRONG CURRENTS, POOR VISIBILITY, VIOLENT STORMS IN SEASON, AND LOW, LOW BITS OF LAND. THE BONEYARD OF MANY A SHIP AND A TREASURE HUNTER'S PARADISE.

WE MAKE A STOP AT *Long Key Bight*. FURTHER WEST, BOOT KEY HARBOR, A SPACIOUS NATURAL ANCHORAGE WITH A MARINA ASHORE, IS A POWERFUL MAGNET FOR CRUISING BOATS (MANY FIND IT HARD TO LEAVE, AND BARNACLES GROW ON THEIR ANCHOR RODES). WE FIND IT TOO CROWDED FOR COMFORT, SO AFTER VISITING AMONGST THE FLEET TO CATCH UP ON NEWS OF CRUISING FRIENDS, WE SET SAIL AGAIN, FOR AN EXCITING STOP AT REMOTE LOOE KEY, ON THE EDGE OF THE GULF STREAM. THERE, WE WERE TOLD BY MARINE BIOLOGISTS AT THE UNIVERSITY OF MIAMI, WE WILL FIND ONE OF THE LAST RICH BEDS OF QUEEN CONCH IN ALL THE KEYS.* WE NOT ONLY SEE CONCH, BUT STINGRAYS, BARRA- CUDA, AND A BIG BROWN NURSE SHARK.

LOOE KEY

TO COMPLETE A GOOD DAY, *SEA WIND* TREATS US TO A FINE SAIL PAST SUGARLOAF KEY. PORPS ESCORT US ON THE LEG IN TO KEY WEST, ROLLING AND PLAYING TOGETHER IN THE BOW WAVE.

*THIS EDIBLE ANIMAL ONCE OCCURRED IN SUCH NUMBERS THAT IT LENT ITS NAME TO THE EARLY INHABITANTS, WHO ALMOST ATE IT TO EXTINCTION. NOW, BELATEDLY, IT IS PROTECTED BY LAW, AND MAY MAKE A COMEBACK.

KEY WEST

The TURNING BASIN, NORTHWEST OF KEY WEST IN THE LEE OF WISTERIA ISLAND (CHRIST-MAS TREE ISLAND) OFFERS AN ANCHORAGE, BUT WE CONSIDER THE CURRENTS, THE TALES OF DINGHY, OAR AND/OR MOTOR THEFT, AND DECIDE WE'LL ENJOY THE "CONCH REPUBLIC" MORE IF AT A MARINA IN GARRISON BIGHT.

Though COVERED WITH A TACKY GLAZE, KEY WEST'S UNDERLYING CHARM SHOWS THROUGH. IT'S BEEN BOOM OR BUST THROUGHOUT ITS HISTORY. WRECKING, SALTMAKING, SPONGING, FISHING – A VALUABLE MILITARY OUTPOST IN THE DAYS WHEN SHIPPING LANES WERE SO IMPORTANT. BOOM TIMES WHEN THE WAR IN CUBA (1868) BROUGHT CUBAN CIGAR MAKERS. BUST WHEN LABOR TROUBLES CAUSED THEM TO MOVE ON TO TAMPA. (THERE'S STILL A LARGE CUBAN COMMUNITY, SPORADICALLY ENLARGED BY WAVES OF POLITICAL REFUGEES.) HARD TIMES DURING THE GREAT DEPRESSION AND THE DESTRUCTION OF FLAGLER'S RAILROAD BY THE 1935 HURRICANE. 1938 SAW THE OVERSEAS HIGHWAY COMPLETED AND THE CREATION OF A NAVY SUBMARINE BASE. THE NAVY BUILT THE PIPELINE THAT STILL BRINGS FRESH WATER FROM THE MAINLAND, THUS SUPPLYING THE ESSENTIAL INGREDIENT FOR THE PRESENT BOOM TIME – TOURISM. (THERETOFORE, RAIN WATER WAS THE ONLY SOURCE.)

CUBA

—106—

LONG A REFUGE
FOR ARTISTS AND WRITERS,
KEY WEST IS ALSO A HANG-
OUT FOR GAYS, LOST SOULS
COLLEGE KIDS, AND MANY,
MANY TOURISTS.

WE ROAM THE QUAINT
STREETS ABSORBING THE
ATMOSPHERE WITH ITS
BLEND OF CARIBBEAN,
AMERICAN AND SPANISH
CULTURES. THE OLD PLACES
ARE DEAR; SOME RESTORED,
SOME FALLING DOWN. A

HEMINGWAY'S HOUSE

SIDEWALK CAFÉ ON DUVAL ST. TREATS US TO CUBAN COOKING
WHILE WE WATCH THE PASSING PARADE. WE VISIT THE FINE
LITTLE AQUARIUM AND MARTELLO EAST (AFTER CAPE MORTELLA IN
CORSICA), A CIVIL WAR FORT BUILT TO RESEMBLE MEDITERRANEAN
FORTIFICATIONS HAVING A CENTRAL TOWER SURROUNDED BY A THICK-
WALLED STRUCTURE.   **SPANISH GOLD** —
DREDGED UP FROM WRECKS IN THE KEYS — IS ON DISPLAY
IN MORE THAN ONE MUSEUM, STIRRING OUR MEMORIES OF
HISTORY AND THE SPANISH MAIN.

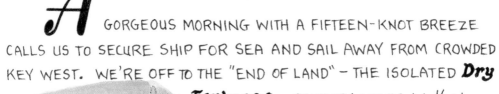

A GORGEOUS MORNING WITH A FIFTEEN-KNOT BREEZE CALLS US TO SECURE SHIP FOR SEA AND SAIL AWAY FROM CROWDED KEY WEST. WE'RE OFF TO THE "END OF LAND" – THE ISOLATED **Dry Tortugas** – SEVENTY MILES W. ½ N. (275°) FROM KEY WEST. AN OVER-NIGHT STOP AT UNINHABITED WOMAN KEY GIVES US A NICE LEE FROM THE WIND, WHICH HAS VEERED INTO THE NOR' EAST. THE ISLAND HAS A FINE LOOK WITH LONG, WHITE BEACHES – A PERFECT COUNTERPOINT TO KEY WEST. WE'RE GLAD TO BE AT ANCHOR AGAIN AND MR. BILL HAS A WILD NIGHT OF FREEDOM ON DECK, CAVORTING ABOUT WITH THE WIND RUFFLING HIS FUR.

SEA WIND IS AWAY AGAIN AT DAWN WITH A ROUSING NOR'EASTER. WE REEF THE MAIN AND USE THE SMALL JIB. AN OCEAN PASSAGE ON THIS SPARKLER OF A DAY TAKES US PAST THE MAR-QUESAS KEYS, THE QUICK-

SANDS, REBECCA SHOALS, AND SO ON TO THE TORTUGAS, WHERE WE SAIL IN TO ANCHOR IN THE LEE OF LONG KEY BY LATE AFTERNOON. WIDE OPEN VISTAS OF SEA AND SKY PREDOMINATE.

IMPOSING *Ft. Jefferson*

IS BUILT AROUND THE PERIMETER OF GARDEN KEY, ENCLOSING SEVEN-
TEEN ACRES. CONSTRUCTION BEGAN IN 1846 AND CONTINUED FOR
THIRTY YEARS. DURING THAT TIME, THE DEVELOPMENT OF RODMAN
GUNS (AFTER A U.S. ARMY CAPTAIN) –
RIFLED CANNON FIRING MORE POWER-
FUL SHELLS – MADE THE UNFINISHED
STRONGHOLD OBSOLETE: SHIPS
CARRYING SUCH GUNS COULD RE-
DUCE EVEN THIS MASSIVE STRUC-
TURE. NEVER UNDER SIEGE, IT WAS
USED AS A PRISON, A NAVAL BASE,
AND AN OBSERVATION POST. THOUGH
IT BECAME A NATIONAL MONUMENT
IN 1935, IT WAS NEGLECTED FOR
MANY YEARS AND SUBJECT TO VAN-
DALISM BY FISHERMEN, SMUGGLERS,
AND EVEN YACHTSMEN. TODAY
IT'S THE DRY TORTUGAS NATIONAL
PARK, RANGERS IN RESIDENCE.
THE FORT IS SLOWLY CRUMBLING
AWAY, BUT IS AN ABSOLUTELY
MAGNIFICENT PIECE OF ARCHI-
TECTURE.

RODMAN GUN

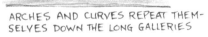

ARCHES AND CURVES REPEAT THEM-
SELVES DOWN THE LONG GALLERIES

THE LASTING VALUE OF THIS OFFSHORE BIT OF LAND AND REEF IS IN THE CLEAR UN-SPOILED BEAUTY OF ITS WATERS AND THE PROLIFERATION OF BIRD AND SEA LIFE. WE SPEND HOURS IN THE WATER OBSERVING CONCH, LOBSTER, CRABS, AND MANY KINDS OF FISH, ALL PROTECTED FROM HUMAN PREDATION HERE WITHIN THE PARK BOUNDARIES.

WE'VE HAD A LONG SPELL OF GOOD WEATHER. THE NORTHERS HAVE BEEN MODERATE. WE KEEP OUR EARS TUNED TO WEATHER REPORTS: THIS IS AN EXPOSED AND LONELY OFFSHORE SPOT. ON A PREVIOUS VISIT (DURING HURRICANE SEASON), WE WERE NOT SO FORTUNATE. A TROPICAL DE-PRESSION MOVED UP FROM THE YUCATAN CHANNEL AND STALLED. WE HAD DAYS OF TWENTY, THIRTY, AND FORTY-KNOT WINDS, WITH INTERMITTENT RAIN, SOME-TIMES TORRENTIAL. IT WAS TOO ROUGH TO ROW THE DINK ASHORE. COM-MERCIAL FISHERMEN SEEKING

TORTUGA-
SPANISH FOR TURTLE

GREEN
SEA TURTLE

SHELTER OVERCROWDED THE LITTLE ANCHORAGE, OCCASIONALLY
DRAGGING THEIR HOMEMADE ANCHORS. WHILE WE LAY NERVOUSLY
TO TWO ANCHORS, THE STORM HOVERED OVER THE ISLAND FOR
ALMOST TWO WEEKS. ONE DAY TWENTY-TWO INCHES OF RAIN
FELL ON THE FORT, DRIVING THE RANGERS FROM THEIR ACCOM-
MODATIONS. WE LOST COUNT OF THE NUMBER OF TIMES THE
DINGHY HAD TO BE BAILED TO KEEP IT FROM SWAMPING. HARDLY
DRY THEN, THESE TORTUGAS.

    WE RELUCTANTLY LEAVE THIS BEAUTIFUL REMOTE ANCHORAGE
FOR *Flamingo*, AT THE SOUTHERN TIP OF FLORIDA, TO CONTINUE
OUR COASTAL CRUISING. THIS PASSAGE IS 110 NAUTICAL MILES
AND SINCE DAYLIGHT IS REQUIRED FOR THE SHALLOW APPROACHES
TO CAPE SABLE AND FLORIDA BAY, WE SAIL OVERNIGHT, USING
THE SEARCHLIGHT TO AVOID FOULING THE THOUSANDS OF STONE
CRAB TRAP FLOATS THAT LITTER OUR PATH. AT
DAWN CAPE SABLE IS LOW ON THE PORT BOW
AND A CHARTED MARKER FINE ON THE
STARBOARD.

$\mathcal{W}$E ARE ON THE DOORSTEP OF THE **Everglades**, THAT HUGE INUNDATED PLAIN DOMINATED BY SAW GRASS MARSHES PUNCTUATED WITH LITTLE HAMMOCKS OF HARDWOOD TREES. BOTH THE EAST AND WEST COASTS OF SOUTH FLORIDA ARE SLIGHTLY ELEVATED, LEAVING THE GREAT TROUGH OF THE EVER-GLADES BETWEEN. IN THE DAYS TO COME, *SEA WIND* WILL TRAVEL ALONG THE SOUTH, WEST AND NORTH EDGES OF THESE SHRINKING EVERGLADES, WHOSE WATER IS BEING STOLEN AND POLLUTED BY FLORIDA'S SWELLING POPULATION AND AGRICULTURE. WE WILL BE ESPECIALLY ALERT TO THE WILD PLACES AND CREATURES IN THIS AILING GIANT SYSTEM, AWARE THAT IF WE PASS THIS WAY AGAIN IN A FEW YEARS, WE MAY NOT SEE THEM AT ALL.

STUART

LAKE OKEECHOBEE

W. PALM BEACH

FT. MYERS

THE EVERGLADES

NAPLES   TAMIAMI TRAIL

FT. LAUDER-DALE

EVERGLADES CITY

MIAMI

EVERGLADES NATIONAL PARK

$\mathcal{N}$

$\mathcal{S}$

SHARP-TOOTHED SAW GRASS - SEDGE FAMILY

FLAMINGO

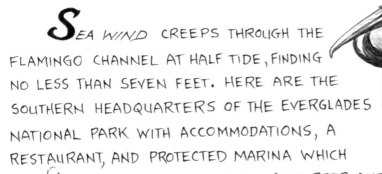

SEA WIND CREEPS THROUGH THE
FLAMINGO CHANNEL AT HALF TIDE, FINDING
NO LESS THAN SEVEN FEET. HERE ARE THE
SOUTHERN HEADQUARTERS OF THE EVERGLADES
NATIONAL PARK WITH ACCOMMODATIONS, A
RESTAURANT, AND PROTECTED MARINA WHICH
SUPPLIES US WITH FUEL, COLD BEER, AND A SLIP. WE
SHARE THE DOCK WITH OVERLY
TAME GULLS AND PELICANS.
DURING OUR STAY, WE
HIKE, BIRD WATCH, AND EX-
PLORE UP
FLAMINGO
CANAL BY
DINGHY TO COOT
BAY. MANY BIRDS,
INCLUDING A PINK IBIS WHICH (WE'RE
INFORMED LATER) IS A HYBRID. WE TREAT
OURSELVES TO A RESTAURANT MEAL.
MAINTENANCE TIME FOR MR. GRAY
MARINE, IN WHOSE HEAD A FINE CRACK HAS
APPEARED. THE FIX CONSISTS OF GRINDING
A LITTLE TROUGH
ON TOP OF THE
CRACK AND
CAULKING IT WITH THE
SKIPPER'S FAVORITE PUTTY,
MARINE TEX. THIS TEMPO-
RARY MEASURE WE HOPE
WILL HOLD UNTIL THE

COOT BAY

FLAMINGO CANAL

WILDERNESS WATERWAY

FLAMINGO

— 113 —

RIGHT TIME AND PLACE FOR A PROPER SOLUTION.* WHEN WE
JOKE ABOUT *SEA WIND* STAYING AFLOAT BECAUSE OF MARINE TEX,
THERE'S SOME TRUTH IN IT, AS THIS VERSATILE PRODUCT
HAS REPAIRED EVERYTHING ABOARD FROM POT
HANDLES TO THROUGH-HULL FITTINGS.

ONE BRIGHT MORNING WE
SET SAIL TO ROUND CAPE SABLE AND
HEAD NORTH. THERE'S THE
TANTALIZING POSSIBILITY OF
ANCHORING OFF ISOLATED MIDDLE
CAPE....VISIONS OF CHOICE BEACH-
COMBING DANCE IN OUR HEADS.
THERE'S EVEN THE CHANCE OF SIGHTING
ONE OF THE RARE FLORIDA PANTHERS
REPORTED TO FREQUENT THIS CAPE. AS
WE ROUND EAST CAPE, HOWEVER, A
WNW BREEZE SPRINGS UP, AND MAKES ENOUGH SURF ALONG
THE SHORE TO DETER US FROM A LANDING.

THE **Little Shark River** BECOMES OUR NEW GOAL. AT
THE ENTRANCE, THERE ARE SHOALS
TO STARBOARD, SO WE HUG THE
GREEN MARKER. WE ANCHOR
FAR ENOUGH UP THE RIVER TO
CLOSE OFF THE OPEN GULF. IT'S
PLEASANT TO BE IN A TREE-LINED
CREEK AGAIN. TIME TO RELAX IN THE
COCKPIT AND LOOK AROUND AT THE LARGEST
MANGROVES WE'VE EVER SEEN — MUST BE SIXTY

* MONTHS LATER A MECHANIC IN A SMALL FLORIDA TOWN FINDS US A RE-
PLACEMENT HEAD FROM A SCRAPPED ENGINE.

-114-

FEET TALL. ON A MUDBANK NEAR-
BY A RACCOON SCRATCHES FOR A
LIVING. TWO EXOTIC ROSEATE
SPOONBILLS, A WHITE IBIS, AND
THE USUAL GREAT BLUE HERON SHARE
OUR ANCHORAGE.

THE OTHER SIDE OF THE COIN IS
PRESENTED TO US WHEN A PARK
RANGER IN A SPEED BOAT
CIRCLES WARILY BEFORE
COMING ALONGSIDE FOR A
GAM. OBVIOUS ON HIS DASH-
BOARD IS A PISTOL; A
SHOTGUN LEANS AGAINST THE
CONSOLE. HE ACCEPTS A CUP OF
TEA AND TALKS ABOUT THE IRONY
OF BEING TRAINED AS A NATURALIST, BUT FUNCTIONING
AS A POLICEMAN. "THERE ARE SO MANY HIDDEN AND
ISOLATED STREAMS AND WATERWAYS IN THE GLADES,
IT'S BECOME A FAVORITE PLACE FOR DRUG SMUGGLERS.
YOU NEVER KNOW WHAT YOU MIGHT FIND WHEN YOU ROUND
A BEND IN MANGROVE COUNTRY."

IN SPITE OF THIS UNSETTLING INFORMATION, AND IN-
TRIGUED BY THE CHART'S MANY WATERCOURSES, WE WANT TO
EXPLORE UP THE LITTLE SHARK AND SHARK RIVERS TO FRESH-
WATER *Tarpon Bay* - TWELVE MILES INLAND. THIS IS AS DEEP
INTO THE "OLD" GLADES AS A KEEL VESSEL CAN PENETRATE.

LITTLE SHARK RIVER

WE'LL BE RUNNING PART OF THE WILDERNESS WATERWAY, WHICH FOLLOWS INLAND STREAMS AND BAYS FROM FLAMINGO TO EVERGLADES CITY. IT'S USED BY CAMPERS IN CANOES AND SMALL BOATS. *SEA WIND* HAS A BEAUTIFUL, THOUGH CHILLY RUN THROUGH WILD FLORIDA COUNTRY. ONE BRIEF GROUNDING OCCURS WHILE WATCHING A BASKING ALLIGATOR.

TARPON BAY, SHAPED LIKE A HANDPRINT,

INVITES A DINGHY EXPLORE. FROM ITS MANY WATERY FINGERS, WE CHOOSE AVACADO CREEK, WANTING TO HAVE A LOOK AT *CANEPATCH*, AN INDIAN MOUND OR KITCHEN MIDDEN NAMED ON THE CHART. AS WE RUN THE NARROWING STREAM WE THINK OF THE CALUSA INDIANS WHO LIVED IN THIS WET WILDERNESS — THEIR LAST REFUGE AND RETREAT FROM EUROPEAN INVADERS. INDEED WE FEEL PRETTY REMOVED FROM CIVILIZATION UNTIL WE COME UPON *CANEPATCH* WITH ITS CAMPSITE AND OBTRUSIVE FIBERGLASS PORTABLE TOILET.*

NEVERTHELESS, A LOVELY, TANGLED SPOT IT IS WITH LOTS OF FRUIT TREES (GUAVA, WATER LEMON, BANANA). IT MUST BE BEASTLY WITH HEAT AND BUGS IN THE

* WE PONDER WHETHER THIS SCENIC POLLUTION IS A VIABLE TRADE OFF AGAINST THE SUPPOSED BIOLOGICAL POLLUTION OF A FEW WILDERNESS CAMPERS. THE MOTORIZED "HONEY BARGE" THAT EMPTIES THESE TOILETS IS ITSELF A KIND OF POLLUTION.

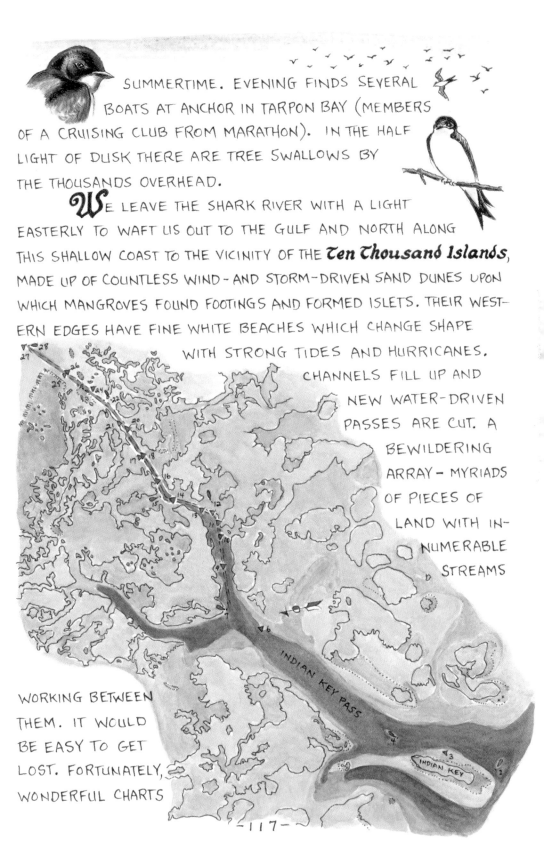

SUMMERTIME. EVENING FINDS SEVERAL BOATS AT ANCHOR IN TARPON BAY (MEMBERS OF A CRUISING CLUB FROM MARATHON). IN THE HALF LIGHT OF DUSK THERE ARE TREE SWALLOWS BY THE THOUSANDS OVERHEAD.

*W*E LEAVE THE SHARK RIVER WITH A LIGHT EASTERLY TO WAFT US OUT TO THE GULF AND NORTH ALONG THIS SHALLOW COAST TO THE VICINITY OF THE *Ten Thousand Islands*, MADE UP OF COUNTLESS WIND- AND STORM-DRIVEN SAND DUNES UPON WHICH MANGROVES FOUND FOOTINGS AND FORMED ISLETS. THEIR WESTERN EDGES HAVE FINE WHITE BEACHES WHICH CHANGE SHAPE WITH STRONG TIDES AND HURRICANES. CHANNELS FILL UP AND NEW WATER-DRIVEN PASSES ARE CUT. A BEWILDERING ARRAY — MYRIADS OF PIECES OF LAND WITH INNUMERABLE STREAMS WORKING BETWEEN THEM. IT WOULD BE EASY TO GET LOST. FORTUNATELY, WONDERFUL CHARTS

INDIAN KEY PASS

INDIAN KEY

AND WELL-KEPT BUOYS SHOW THE WAY. OUR WAY IS INDIAN KEY PASS, THROUGH CHOKO-LOSKEE BAY AND UP THE BARRON RIVER TO **Everglades City**, LOCATED ON THE NORTH-WESTERN EDGE OF EVERGLADES NATIONAL PARK. THIS SMALL TOWN SHOWS AN ATTRAC-TIVE FACE TO THE WATER. *SEA WIND* TIES UP AT THE ROD AND GUN CLUB. THE OLD LODGE HAS A WONDERFUL DARK PANELED INTERIOR COM-PLETE WITH MOUNTED FISH AND STUFFED GAME. WE TAKE A WALK ABOUT BUT SOON RETREAT TO *SEA WIND*'S INTERIOR. ONE THING EVERGLADES CITY HAS AND THAT'S PLENTY OF MOSQUITOES!

A QUIET SAIL AROUND CAPE ROMANO AND NORTH TO GORDON PASS BRINGS US TO CHARMING **Naples** AND A RETURN TO

BUSTLING CIVILIZATION. THE MUNICIPAL MARINA'S DOCKS ARE FULL, FORCING US TO ANCHOR AND USE THE DINGHY. THE TINY HARBOR IS IN THE HEART OF TOWN, SO WE SPEND A DAY ASHORE BEING FOOT TOURISTS.

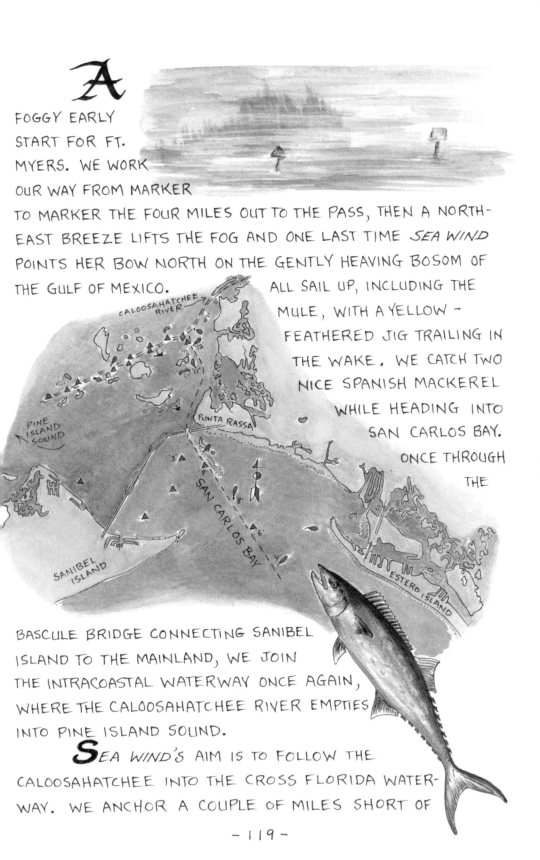

A FOGGY EARLY START FOR FT. MYERS. WE WORK OUR WAY FROM MARKER TO MARKER THE FOUR MILES OUT TO THE PASS, THEN A NORTH-EAST BREEZE LIFTS THE FOG AND ONE LAST TIME *SEA WIND* POINTS HER BOW NORTH ON THE GENTLY HEAVING BOSOM OF THE GULF OF MEXICO. ALL SAIL UP, INCLUDING THE MULE, WITH A YELLOW-FEATHERED JIG TRAILING IN THE WAKE. WE CATCH TWO NICE SPANISH MACKEREL WHILE HEADING INTO SAN CARLOS BAY. ONCE THROUGH THE BASCULE BRIDGE CONNECTING SANIBEL ISLAND TO THE MAINLAND, WE JOIN THE INTRACOASTAL WATERWAY ONCE AGAIN, WHERE THE CALOOSAHATCHEE RIVER EMPTIES INTO PINE ISLAND SOUND.

SEA *WIND'S* AIM IS TO FOLLOW THE CALOOSAHATCHEE INTO THE CROSS FLORIDA WATER-WAY. WE ANCHOR A COUPLE OF MILES SHORT OF

FT. MYERS JUST OFF THE WATERWAY NEAR MARKER "60". WE WANT TO RE-LAX, POACH OUR FISH, AND LET THE EVER-GLADES EXPERIENCE SOAK IN. BEFORE THESE MEMORIES ARE COOL, HOWEVER, WE BEGIN TO ANTICIPATE CRUISING THROUGH THE MIDDLE OF FLORIDA.

A TIE UP AT THE CITY YACHT BASIN IN **Ft.Myers** PROVIDES ACCESS TO THE DOWNTOWN AREA. ORIGI-NALLY A FORT IN THE SEMINOLE WARS, FT. MYERS BECAME A COW TOWN - WHERE CATTLE WERE ROUNDED UP FOR SHIP-MENT. IN 1871 MORE THAN A HUNDRED SCHOONER LOADS OF CATTLE WERE SENT OFF TO CUBA AND THE BAHAMAS. THOMAS EDISON DEVELOPED AN ESTATE ON THE RIVER AND A HIGH POINT FOR US IS A TOUR THROUGH THE BEAUTIFULLY - KEPT GROUNDS (ALL KINDS OF IMPORTED TREES AND PLANTS), THE OLD HOME, LABORATORY, AND MU - SEUM HOUSING EDISON'S INVENTIONS.

*I*N 1882 THE FIRST DREDGE WAS ASSEMBLED HERE AND RUN UP THE CALOOSAHATCHEE RIVER TO START DRAIN-ING THE EVERGLADES. CLOSE BEHIND THE DREDGING OPERATIONS CAME BOOM TIMES FOR HOMESTEADERS, FARMERS, AND DEVELOPERS. THOSE TIMES ARE STILL GOING ON.

$\mathcal{T}$OPPED UP WITH FUEL, WATER, AND FRESH SUPPLIES, SEA WIND HEADS UP THE CALOOSAHATCHEE. AHEAD IS YET ANOTHER FACET OF FLORIDA TO EXPERIENCE — ONE AWAY FROM THE TOURIST ATTRACTIONS OF THE COASTS, AND SUBTLY DIFFERENT FROM THAT OTHER INLAND WATERCOURSE, THE ST. JOHNS RIVER. AGRICULTURAL FLORIDA SURROUNDS THE OKEECHOBEE WATERWAY, AND THE BIG LAKE IN THE CENTER IS REALLY BIG — THE SECOND LARGEST FRESH WATER LAKE WITHIN THE U.S.

$\mathcal{W}$E'RE RUSHED INTO THE NARROWER WATERS OF THE **Caloosahatchee River** BY A STRONG WEST WIND. MR. GRAY IS AT THE READY FOR BRIDGES AND THE FRANKLIN LOCK (AT OLGA). THEN WE'RE IN THE PRETTIEST STRETCH OF WINDING RIVER. LIVE OAKS APPEAR, AND ORANGE GROVES AND COW PASTURAGE. ISLETS WITH DEEP WATER BEHIND THEM, FORMED WHEN THE RIVER WAS STRAIGHTENED, ARE NUMEROUS. THESE OXBOWS MAKE APPEALING ANCHORAGES. WE FIND A BEAUT BELOW DENAUD.

WATER HYACINTHS CLOG THE ENTRANCE. THE SKIPPER LASSOS SOME FROM THE DINGHY, PULLS THEM ASIDE TO LET *SEA WIND* SLIP THROUGH. THEY THEN DRIFT BACK, LEAVING US IN AN ENCLOSED GREEN GROTTO. GRASSES, WATER LILLIES, PICKEREL WEED, CATTAILS IN THE SHALLOWS. TREES OVERHANG THE WATER. SCENT OF ORANGE BLOSSOMS. THE BACK-SIDE OF THE ISLET HAS A BROKEN-DOWN DOCK; ASHORE THE WRECK OF A SHACK. THIS QUIET PLACE SATISFIES US MIGHTILY. TIME TO CLEAN *SEA WIND*, VARNISH HER OUTSIDE TEAK AND POLISH UP HER STAINLESS STEEL PULPIT AND RUB RAIL WHILE BELOW THE GALLEY COPPER IS SHINED AS WELL.

PICKEREL WEED

WATER LILY

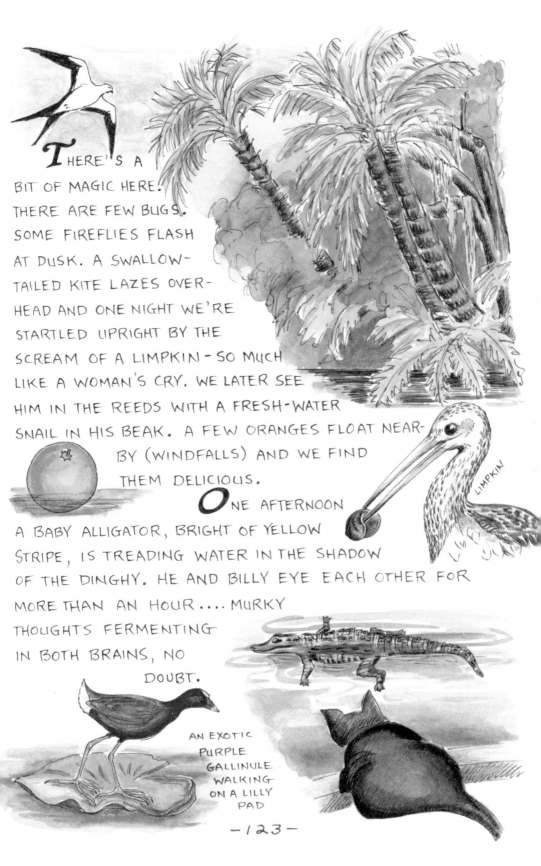

THERE'S A BIT OF MAGIC HERE! THERE ARE FEW BUGS. SOME FIREFLIES FLASH AT DUSK. A SWALLOW-TAILED KITE LAZES OVERHEAD AND ONE NIGHT WE'RE STARTLED UPRIGHT BY THE SCREAM OF A LIMPKIN - SO MUCH LIKE A WOMAN'S CRY. WE LATER SEE HIM IN THE REEDS WITH A FRESH-WATER SNAIL IN HIS BEAK. A FEW ORANGES FLOAT NEAR-BY (WINDFALLS) AND WE FIND THEM DELICIOUS.

LIMPKIN

ONE AFTERNOON A BABY ALLIGATOR, BRIGHT OF YELLOW STRIPE, IS TREADING WATER IN THE SHADOW OF THE DINGHY. HE AND BILLY EYE EACH OTHER FOR MORE THAN AN HOUR.... MURKY THOUGHTS FERMENTING IN BOTH BRAINS, NO DOUBT.

AN EXOTIC PURPLE GALLINULE WALKING ON A LILLY PAD

*F*ROM OUR QUIET POOL WE SEE WATERWAY TRAVELERS —
YACHTS, BARGES AND TUGS, FISHERMEN.
  *A*LL IDYLLS MUST END. THE WATER HYACINTHS ARE
HAULED ASIDE AND
WE SURRENDER OUR
Green Mansions
TO THE BABY ALLIGATOR, WHO'S LURKING BEHIND A LILY PAD
THIS MORNING. A SHORT RUN BRINGS US TO THE ***La Belle***
CITY DOCK. OUR BICYCLES TAKE US AROUND
THIS OLD RIVER TOWN FOR THE
NECESSARIES — LAUNDRY,
SHOPPING — AND THE USUAL
RUBBER-NECKING. SPECIAL-
TIES ARE LOCAL HONEY AND
SWAMP CABBAGE (HEARTS OF
PALM). HERE AND AT OTHER
TOWNS ALONG THE RIVER WHERE
CATTLEMEN MEET, LOTS OF COWBOY
BOOTS AND STETSONS ARE IN EVIDENCE.
THE MATE BRINGS HOME GROUND
SIRLOIN AND TURKEY BREAST. THESE
ARE STUFFED INTO CANNING JARS
AND PRESSURE COOKED; PROVISIONS
FOR SUMMERTIME CRUISING IN THE
BAHAMAS.
  *U*NDER WAY
FOR ***Moore Haven***, WHICH IS PERCHED ON THE EDGE OF
LAKE OKEECHOBEE, WE'RE LIFTED IN THE ORTONA LOCK
(SECOND LOCK ON THE CALOOSAHATCHEE SIDE OF THE CROSS
FLORIDA WATERWAY). HOW MUCH ONE IS LIFTED DEPENDS

ON THE CURRENT HEIGHT OF THE
LAKE. PART OF THE DAY IS SPENT AT
THE MOORE HAVEN MUNICIPAL DOCK. A TINY
PARK ON THE WATERFRONT FEATURES A
VENERABLE LONE CYPRESS TREE WHICH HAS
SERVED AS A NAVIGATIONAL AID FOR BOATMEN
SINCE EARLY IN THE CENTURY. ACROSS THE STREET IN THE
LIBRARY, VOLUNTEER LADIES ARE SELLING PACKAGES OF
LOCALLY-GROWN RICE DONATED FOR FUND
RAISING. SUBSEQUENTLY WE FIND IT SO
FLAVORFUL WE WISH WE'D GOTTEN
MORE. BIG BUSINESS HERE IS FARM
PRODUCE, CATFISH, AND SUGAR-
CANE. THE LATTER, INTRODUCED
AFTER WORLD WAR 1, EXPLODED
IN THE 60'S WHEN THE IMPORT OF
CUBA'S SUGAR WAS CUT OFF. NOW
IT DOMINATES FARM COUNTRY
AROUND THE LAKE.

LAKE
OKEECHOBEE
LOCK
MOORE HAVEN
BRIDGE

UNWILLING TO SPEND ANOTHER
NIGHT AT DOCKS, WE PERUSE THE CHART FOR A NEARBY ANCHOR-
AGE. THE DOCKLINES ARE RETRIEVED AND
SEA WIND
LOCKS THROUGH
THE THIRD LOCK
ON THIS SIDE
OF THE LAKE.
TO PORT IS A
STRETCH OF LITTLE-USED
CANAL BEHIND SPOIL ISLANDS.

MOORE HAVEN
BASCULE BRIDGE

A MILE OR SO UP THIS CANAL WE DROP THE HOOK IN A PLEASANT WILD-FEELING SPOT. A BIG ALLIGATOR DECORATES THE BANK AND A MANATEE ROLLS UNDER OUR BOWS AT DUSK. AFTER SUPPER THE FROG

CHORUS COMES ON— A DEAFENING CACOPHONY. BILLY STAYS ON DECK LISTENING FAR INTO THE NIGHT. *We* THINK ABOUT *Lake Okeechobee*.

THIRTY-FIVE MILES LONG AND THIRTY-ONE MILES WIDE (SEVEN HUNDRED SQ. MI.). IN ITS NATURAL STATE, THE LAKE WAS FULL IN THE RAINY SEASON AND SHRANK BACK IN THE DRY. IT REGULARLY OVERFLOWED ITS SHORES, SPREADING ITS NUTRIENTS TO THE SOUTHERN SAW GRASS PLAIN. IN 1926 AND 1928 DEVASTATING STORMS SWEPT THROUGH THE AREA ON TOP OF THE ALREADY RAIN-SWOLLEN LAKE. HURRICANE WINDS DROVE THE WATER ACROSS THE SURROUNDING

LANDS, DESTROYING TOWNS, CROPS, AND EIGHTEEN HUNDRED PEOPLE. THESE DISASTERS RESULTED IN THE CONSTRUCTION OF A VAST SYSTEM OF LEVEES, CANALS, LOCKS, SPILLWAYS, AND HURRICANE GATES. EARTHWORKS WERE THROWN UP EIGHTY-FIVE MILES ALONG THE EAST, SOUTH, AND WEST SIDES OF THE LAKE. THESE IMPOUNDED WATERS ARE NOW USED TO IRRIGATE A VAST AGRICULTURE AND SERVE THE BURGEONING POPULATION. THE UNIQUE ECOSYSTEM THESE CONTROLS ARE STARVING IS CALLED, IRONICALLY, THE EVERGLADES. SOMBER THOUGHTS IN A BLACK NIGHT.

EARLY MORNING MISTS RISE FROM THE WATER. BIRD CALLS IN THE MARSHES AND THE ROAR OF FISHERMEN'S AIR BOATS COMPETE FOR OUR ATTENTION. UP! UP! IT'S TIME TO BE AWAY! SHALL WE TAKE THE DIRECT ROUTE ACROSS THE LAKE? NO. THE RIM ROUTE, SOUTH ABOUT, HOLDS MUCH MORE INTEREST, SINCE FOR TWENTY-THREE MILES IT RUNS BETWEEN THE MAINLAND AND SPOIL ISLANDS. TREES LINE BOTH SIDES, GIVING A NICE FEELING OF PROTECTION. PINES AND MELALEUCA ON THE LAKE SIDE—CASUARINAS ON THE MAINLAND. THE MELALEUCA, A RELATIVE OF THE AUSTRALIAN EUCALYPTUS, WAS INTRODUCED IN THE EARLY NINETEEN HUNDREDS BY DEVELOPERS WHO SCATTERED SEEDS OVER THE EVERGLADES FROM LOW-FLYING AIRPLANES.

THE PURPOSE WAS TO AID IN DRYING THE SWAMPLANDS — MELA-
LEUCAS CONSUME A LOT OF GROUND WATER. UNFORTUNATELY,
IN AREAS WHERE ESTABLISHED, THE LAND SUPPORTS LITTLE
ELSE. ANOTHER BLOW TO THE NATIVE FLORA.

THIS BECOMES ONE OF
OUR BEST WATERWAY
DAYS EVER, WITH AN
ABUNDANCE OF BIRDS TO
OBSERVE. HERONS: LITTLE
BLUE, GREAT BLUE, GREAT
WHITE, LOUISIANA, LITTLE GREEN,
YELLOW-CROWNED NIGHT; VUL-
TURES (BOTH KINDS); CROWS
(BOTH KINDS); CATTLE EGRET,
WHITE AND GLOSSY IBIS, COMMON
GALLINULE, RED-TAILED HAWK,
WOOD STORK, PIED BILLED GREBE,
KINGFISHER, COOT, LIMPKIN, COMMON
FLICKER, SPARROW, AND MANY
ANHINGAS (SNAKEBIRD). FISHERMEN
IN FAST BOATS PASS US, AND WE
PASS SOME WITH QUIET
ELECTRIC TROLLING MOTORS.
BILLY, OUR FERDINAND OF A

CAT, ACCIDENTALLY CATCHES A LARGE DRAGONFLY,
THEN DOESN'T KNOW WHAT TO DO WITH IT. THE
DAY BECOMES HOT ENOUGH TO WARM OUR BONES.
PAST CLEWISTON WITH ITS HURRICANE GATE, AND
LURED ON BY THE TREE-LINED CANAL AHEAD,
WE PASS THROUGH THE CHARMING, DILATORY

HAND-OPERATED
SWING BRIDGE
CONNECTING
TORRY ISLAND

TO THE MAINLAND. CLOUDS ARE BUILDING OVER THE LAKE. MANY
HOUSEBOATS ARE MOORED
AMONG THE SPOIL ISLANDS –
ALL KINDS – FROM TACKY TO
CUTE, NONE VERY ELEGANT.
To PROLONG THE
OKEECHOBEE SPELL, *SEA WIND*
SPENDS ONE MORE NIGHT ON
THE LAKE, SNUGGING UP UNDER A
LAST STRETCH OF SPOIL. IN LATE AFTERNOON, A HUMDINGER
OF A THUNDERSTORM BARRELS THROUGH. *SEA WIND'S* BOW
PEELS OFF AS THE PLOW ANCHOR DRAGS THROUGH
THE SOFT BOTTOM. SKIPPER LETS GO THE
FISHERMAN, WHICH
BRINGS US UP NICELY.

FISHER-
MAN

PLOW

FOR THE NIGHT, WE TAKE A STERN LINE TO A MELA-LEUCA WHICH KEEPS US CLEAR OF THE CHANNEL AND GIVES PEACE OF MIND.

IT'S GREY AND QUIET ON THE OPEN LAKE. THE REMAINING MILES SLIP BY EASILY. WE LOOK BACK ON THE PLACID, PALE FACE OF LAKE OKEECHOBEE UNTIL, WITH A FINE AND FITTING FINALITY, THE GATES OF THE PORT MAYACA LOCK CLOSE BEHIND US. *SEA WIND* DESCENDS INTO THE ST. LUCIE CANAL, AND SOON COMES TO THE

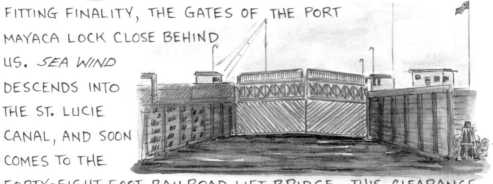

FORTY-EIGHT FOOT RAILROAD LIFT BRIDGE. THIS CLEARANCE DETERMINES WHICH SAILBOATS CAN OR CANNOT PASS THIS WAY. IT LOOKS QUAINT AND NARROW SPANNING THE CHANNEL.

We RUN THE LAST FEW MILES TO STUART WITH A SENSE OF CLOSURE. THIS IS THE END OF A JOURNEY. SOON AFTER THE LAST LOCK HAS LOWERED US INTO THE SOUTH FORK OF THE ST. LUCIE RIVER, WE CROSS OUR SOUTHBOUND TRACK, AND *SEA WIND'S* INTRACOASTAL ODYSSEY IS COMPLETE. AHEAD LIES ANOTHER ADVENTURE.

SEA WIND HAS SHOWN US A UNIQUE SLICE OF AMERICA, RICH IN HISTORY AND CONTAINING SOME OF THE WILDEST HABITATS ALONG THE EASTERN COAST; ENCOUNTERED A VARIETY OF CULTURES; GIVEN US ACCESS TO COSMOPOLITAN CITIES — NORFOLK, CHARLESTON, SAVANNAH, JACKSONVILLE, PALM BEACH, AND MIAMI. WE PASSED OR WERE PASSED BY A VAST SPECTRUM OF WATERCRAFT — TUGS WITH BARGES, SOUND SHRIMPERS, SMALL WORK BOATS OF ALL KINDS, AND OF COURSE, THE INFINITE VARIETY OF YACHTS — BOTH POWER AND SAIL.

THERE ARE SO MANY FACES TO THE WATERWAY THAT NO TWO PASSAGES ALONG IT ARE ALIKE. IT'S DIFFERENT GOING NORTH THAN SOUTH. DIFFERENT DEPENDING ON WEATHER AND SEASON. ONE TRIP BARELY SCRATCHES THE SURFACE OF POSSIBLE PLACES TO EXPLORE, MISSED THE LAST TIME THROUGH, OR LEARNED OF LATER. WE WILL HAVE TO DO IT AGAIN!

Bibliography

BAILEY, ANTHONY, *THE INSIDE PASSAGE.* N.Y., MACMILLAN, 1965.

BALLANTINE, TODD, *TIDELAND TREASURE.* DEERFIELD PUBLISHING, INC., 1983.

BARTRAM, WILLIAM, *THE TRAVELS OF WILLIAM BARTRAM.* N.Y., FACSIMILE LIBRARY, 1940.

BEBLER, JOHN L. & KING, F. WAYNE, *THE AUDUBON SOCIETY FIELD GUIDE TO NORTH AMERICAN REPTILES AND AMPHIBIANS.* N.Y., ALFRED A. KNOPF, 1979.

BLANCHARD, FESSENDEN S., *A CRUISING GUIDE TO THE SOUTHERN COAST.* N.Y., DODD, MEAD & CO., 1964.

————, *A CRUISING GUIDE TO THE INLAND WATERWAY & FLORIDA.* N.Y., DODD, MEAD & CO., 1954.

BROWN, ALEXANDER CROSBY, *JUNIPER WATERWAY.* UNIVERSITY PRESS OF VIRGINIA, 1981.

BULL, JOHN & FARRAND, JOHN JR., *THE AUDUBON SOCIETY FIELD GUIDE TO NORTH AMERICAN BIRDS.* N.Y., ALFRED A. KNOPF, 1977.

BYRD, WILLIAM, *HISTORIES OF THE DIVIDING LINE BETWIXT VA. & NORTH CAROLINA.* N.Y., DOVER PUBLICATIONS, INC., 1967.

CARSTARPHEN, DEE, *THE CONCH BOOK.* VIRGINIA, PEN & INK PRESS, 1982.

CRONKITE, WALTER & ELLIS, RAY, *SOUTH BY SOUTHEAST.* ALABAMA, OXMOOR HOUSE, 1983.

CHAPLIN, CHARLES C. G., *FISHWATCHERS GUIDE.* PA., LIVINGSTON PUBLISHING CO., 1972.

DE HARTOG, JAN, *WATERS OF THE NEW WORLD.* N.Y., ATHENEUM, 1961.

DOUGLAS, MARJORY STONEMAN, *THE EVERGLADES, RIVER OF GRASS.* SARASOTA, FLORIDA, PINEAPPLE PRESS, INC., 1988.

FEDERAL WRITERS' PROJECT OF THE W.P.A., *THE OCEAN HIGHWAY.* N.Y., MODERN AGE BOOKS, 1938.

GOODSON, GAR, *FISHES OF THE ATLANTIC COAST.* CALIFORNIA, MARQUEST COLORGUIDE BOOKS, 1976.

GREENBERG, JERRY & IDAZ, *THE LIVING REEF.* FLORIDA, SEAHAWK PRESS, 1974.

HARGREAVES, DOROTHY & BOB, *TROPICAL TREES.* HAWAII, HARGREAVES CO., INC., 1965.

MID-ATLANTIC WATERWAY GUIDE 1995. ATLANTA, GEORGIA, ARGUS BUSINESS, 1995.

MORRISON, ROBERT H. & LEE, CHRISTINE ECKSTROM, *AMERICAS ATLANTIC ISLES.* WASHINGTON, D.C., THE NATIONAL GEOGRAPHIC SOCIETY, 1981.

NARRATIVE OF A VOYAGE TO THE SPANISH MAIN IN THE SHIP "TWO FRIENDS".
   FLORIDA, UNIVERSITY PRESSES OF FLORIDA, 1978.
NATIONAL ASSOCIATION OF AUDUBON SOCIETIES, BIRDS OF AMERICA.
   N.Y., GARDEN CITY PUBLISHING CO., INC., 1936.
PAPY, FRANK, CRUISING GUIDE TO THE FLORIDA KEYS. SOUTH CAROLINA,
   SELF-PUBLISHED, 1992.
PETERSON, ROGER TORY, A FIELD GUIDE TO THE BIRDS EAST OF THE
   ROCKIES. BOSTON, MA., HOUGHTON MIFFLIN CO., 1980.
PLUMMER, HENRY, THE BOY, ME & THE CAT. MA. HOUGHTON MIFFLIN, 1980.
SOUTHWARD BY THE INSIDE ROUTE. N.Y. RUDDER PUBLISHING CO., 1902.
SOUTHERN WATERWAY GUIDE 1994. ATLANTA, GEORGIA, ARGUS
   BUSINESS, 1994.
STEVENSON, GEORGE B., KEY GUIDE. FLORIDA, SELF-PUBLISHED, 1970.
TEALE, EDWIN WAY, NORTH WITH THE SPRING. N.Y. DODD, MEAD & CO. 1961.
WHITAKER, JOHN O., JR., THE AUDUBON SOCIETY FIELD GUIDE TO NORTH
   AMERICAN MAMMALS. N.Y., ALFRED A. KNOPF, 1980.
ZIM, HERBERT S., & GABRIELSON, IRA N., BIRDS. N.Y., GOLDEN PRESS,
   1956.
———— & SHOEMAKER, HURST H., FISHES. N.Y. GOLDEN PRESS, 1955.
————, A GUIDE TO EVERGLADES NATIONAL PARK & THE NEARBY
   FLORIDA KEYS. N.Y., GOLDEN PRESS, 1960.
———— & HOFFMEISTER, DONALD F., MAMMALS. N.Y. GOLDEN PRESS, 1955.
———— & SMITH, HOBART M., REPTILES & AMPHIBIANS. N.Y., GOLDEN
   PRESS, 1956.

The Author/Artist (AND FIRST MATE) IS DEE CARSTARPHEN. HER SAILING INCLUDES THE COASTS OF CALIFORNIA, MEXICO, WEST COAST OF CENTRAL AMERICA, A TRANSIT OF THE PANAMA CANAL, AND THE CARIBBEAN BASIN WHERE SHE SPENT SEVERAL YEARS IN THE CHARTER BUSINESS. SHE AND STU MET WHEN DEE OWNED A COTTAGE IN THE BAHAMAS AND JOINED HIM ON *SEA WIND* TO SAIL FROM THE COAST OF MAINE TO THE CARIBBEAN AND BACK AGAIN, KEEPING SKETCH LOGS ALONG THE WAY.

Sea Wind's Skipper IS STUART HOPKINS, AN EX-JOURNALIST AND EDITOR FROM CHICAGO, WHO OPTED OUT OF CITY LIFE MANY YEARS AGO WHEN HE BECAME ENAMOURED OF SAILING/CRUISING AND FLED DOWN THE MIGHTY MISSISSIPPI TO SPEND YEARS EXPLORING THE BAHAMAS, CARIBBEAN, BERMUDA, AND THE SOUTH AND EAST COASTS OF THE U.S.

THE BOAT

DESIGNED BY
THOMAS C. GILMER
SEA WIND 30
LOA 30'6" (9.30m)
LWL 24'0" (7.32m)
BEAM 9'3" (2.82m)
DRAFT 4'6" (1.37m)
SAIL AREA 500 ⌀
(46.4m²)
POWER 25 HP
GRAYMARINE
GAS ENGINE